Literacy
Teacher's Book

Year 3

Every effort has been made to trace copyright holders and to obtain their permission for the use of copyright material. The authors and publishers would gladly receive information enabling them to rectify any error or omission in subsequent editions.

Acknowledgements
The authors and publisher are grateful for permission to reproduce the following text:

Josie Smith at the Seaside by Magdalen Nabb published by HarperCollins Publishers Ltd; 'Weather' from First Rhymes by Lucy Coates (illustrated in the original publication by Selina Young), first published in the UK by Orchard Books, a division of the Watts Publishing Group, 96 Leonard Street, London EC2A 4RH; *Chips and Jessie* by Shirley Hughes, published by Bodley Head; *The Battle of Bubble and Squeak* by Philippa Pearce, published by Scholastic Children's Books; *The Birthday Surprise* by Julia Donaldson, published by Ginn; the extract from 'Puppy and I' from When We Were Very Young, published by Methuen Children's Books 1924 (a division of Reed International Books Ltd) reproduced by permission of the Trustees of the Pooh Properties; the extract from 'Rap Connected' from Talking Turkeys by Benjamin Zephaniah, published by Puffin Children's Books; *Indian Legends of the Pacific Northwest* by Ella Clark, published by the University of California, © 1953 The Regents of the University of California, renewed 1981 Ella E. Clark; *On the Run* by Nina Bawden published by Hamish Hamilton, reprinted by permission of Curtis Brown Ltd; *Fantastic Mr Fox* by Roald Dahl, published by Cape; *The BFG* by Roald Dahl, published by Cape; 'The Adventures of Isabel' by Ogden Nash, 1936 renewed, reprinted by permission of Curtis Brown Ltd.

First published 1998, Reprinted 1999

Letts Educational, Schools and Colleges Division,
9–15 Aldine Street, London W12 8AW
Tel: 0181 740 2270   Fax: 0181 740 2280

Text © Louis Fidge

ISBN 1 84085 242 9

Designed by Gecko Limited, Bicester, Oxon
Produced by Ken Vail Graphic Design, Cambridge

Illustrated by Richard Adams (The Inkshed), Kiran Ahmad, Sally Artz, Jonathan Bentley (Beint & Beint), Liz Catchpole, John Eastwood (Maggie Mundy Illustration Agency), David Frankland (Artist Partners), Gecko Limited, Tania Hurt-Newton, Steve Lach, Doreen McGuiness, Robert McPhillips, Shelagh McNicholas, Dave Mostyn, Jan Nesbit, Andrew Warrington, Mark Lawrence, Karen Donnelly

British Library Cataloguing-in-Publication Data
A CIP record for this book is available from the British Library

Printed in Great Britain by Ashford Colour Press

Letts Educational is the trading name of BPP (Letts Educational) Ltd

CONTENTS

The Poster Packs:

- support the teaching of the Literacy Hour
- provide a major teaching/learning focus
- cover a wide range of types of literature, both fiction and non-fiction
- are useful for class, group or independent work
- contain teaching notes offering a wealth of practical ideas
- include activities and suggestions for text, sentence and word level work

Teaching and learning strategies

The posters facilitate a wide range of teaching and learning strategies. They provide:

- a clear focus, allowing you to draw attention to and develop key strategies with the class
- opportunities to demonstrate skills, e.g. on how to read punctuation using a shared text
- opportunities for modelling, e.g. by discussing the features of the texts
- suggestions for scaffolding by offering support and structures for compositional writing
- the means to explain, clarify and discuss texts in a variety of ways at all three levels
- opportunities for questioning and probing understanding so pupils extend their ideas
- a means of initiating and guiding explorations into all areas of language, including grammar, spelling and meaning
- the means to investigate ideas and themes, e.g. to understand, expand on or generalise about underlying text structures
- opportunities to promote discussion and argument, encouraging pupils to voice their opinions, put forward their views, argue a case, or justify a preference
- a chance to develop speaking and listening skills, stimulating and extending pupils' contributions by discussion and evaluation.

Class activities – shared reading and writing

The posters may be used for a variety of purposes in a whole class situation. It is suggested that initially the text is read to the whole class, modelling good reading aloud, emphasising meaning and expression, paying due attention to the punctuation. The passage may be discussed for a variety of purposes.

- The posters may be used to extend reading skills and understanding. Activities may be selected from the text level suggestions for a variety of comprehension activities, encouraging children to read the lines, between and beyond the lines.
- Similarly the passage may be used as a platform for developing compositional writing. Activities may be selected from the writing composition menu. These may be chosen for a variety of reasons, e.g. for the purpose of promoting a class discussion, brainstorming ideas, planning, writing notes, etc., for subsequent use in a group session or as an independent activity.
- The passage on the poster may also be used as a basis for class work at Sentence Level, by selecting appropriate activities from either the 'grammatical awareness' section or the 'sentence construction and punctuation' section.
- At Word Level, the passages on the posters provide many opportunities for focussing on spelling or vocabulary work, by selecting appropriate activities from the relevant sections of the Teacher's Notes.

Guided group activities

The main difference in these sessions is that, whereas in the shared class sessions the emphasis was on modelling appropriate behaviour to the children, in these guided group sessions children are helped to develop their own *independent* reading and writing skills.

The posters are equally useful in the context of smaller group work, following on from the larger class activities. Having read the text previously with the class, it will now be more familiar and thus provide a valuable passage for practising developing reading skills. For example, the text could be read aloud for developing a greater awareness of phrasing, intonation, expression, attention to punctuation, etc. The text could be used for further comprehension activities from the suggestions in the teacher's notes, refining and developing children's abilities to use a variety of reading strategies and cues.

The posters may be used to develop writing tasks introduced earlier with the whole class, e.g. planning a piece of writing to be continued later, working on sentence construction activities, discussing ways of presenting an argument, etc.

Independent work

Independent work will be happening at the same time as the guided group work. A variety of forms of organisation are possible for this work. Independent work may be carried out within the context of ability groups operating on a carousel system, with a rotation of activities for each group during the week, or as completely individual work, e.g. a whole class writing activity based on an earlier shared writing session.

In the shared class activities, the posters will have been used for a wide range of teaching objectives at any of the three levels of text, sentence or word work. The teacher's notes contain a comprehensive range of ideas which are suitable for independent work at each level, using the posters as a starting point. The posters, if not being used by other groups, could be available for reference purposes if necessary. The activities suggested are often not reliant on access to the poster at all.

Independent tasks could cover a wide range of objectives such as:

– independent reading and writing
– spelling activities and practice
– comprehension work
– vocabulary extension and dictionary or thesaurus work

– grammar, punctuation and sentence construction activities
– proof-reading and editing
– reviewing and evaluating work done, etc.

The plenary session

The posters provide an ideal focus for drawing sessions together. The session may be used to:

– refer back to and reinforce earlier teaching points by reference to the poster, helping pupils discuss, reflect upon and evaluate their work
– present pupils' work to the rest of the class
– assess what has been learned in the lesson
– flag up teaching points for future lessons
– praise and encourage achievements.

The relationship between the Posters and the Letts Literacy Activity Books

The posters may be used entirely independently as a resource in their own right, as suggested above. However, to get maximum value from them, they are best used to complement the work in the Letts Literacy Activity Books. The stimulus passages on the posters are exactly the same as those which introduce each unit of work in the Activity Books. The activities are different, however. The combination of both Activity Books and ideas from the Poster Packs thus provides you with an even more extensive range of suggestions from which to select according to your individual situations and the needs of your class.

The texts themselves may be best introduced and discussed with the class, intially using the posters. Pupils could use the Activity Books as well, if you consider this appropriate. (The posters may, of course, also be used as a focus for small group and individual work, as suggested above.)

When not being specifically used as a teaching tool, individual posters could be pinned up in the classroom as part of your on-going classroom display, e.g. as the 'Poster of the week'.

Scope and Sequence for the Activity Book

Text Level	Sentence Level	Word Level
• Story settings	Introducing dialogue	Prefixes
• Shape poetry	Verb tenses	Syllables
• Poetry	Grammatical awareness; Punctuation	Phonemes; Spelling strategies
• Story setting	Presentation of text	Proof-reading for spelling mistakes
• Settings and characters playscripts	General punctuation	Phonemes; Spelling strategies

Writing Focus 1.1   Story structure; Story settings; Shape poems; Plays; Handy hints for writing stories

• Story setting	Speech marks	Words ending with 'le'
• Using a dictionary and thesaurus	Verbs	Synonyms; Alphabetical order
• Main points; Fiction; Non-fiction	Verbs	Verbs ending in 'ing'
• Locating information	Commas in lists	Spelling strategies
• Playscripts	Types of sentences	Phonemes

Writing Focus 1.2   Labelling; Presenting information; Writing reports; Handy hints for checking your work

• Story themes; Key incidents	Common nouns	Singular and plural
• Story themes; Characterisation	Common and collective nouns	Singular and plural
• Characterisation; Story language	Adjectives	Silent letters
• Characterisation	Adjectives	Suffixes
• Performance poetry	Use of 1st and 3rd person; Capitals	Suffixes; Apostrophes (contractions)

Writing Focus 2.1   Story structure; Story sequels; Fairy stories/traditional tales; Handy hints for writing fairy stories

• Characterisation; Story themes	Use of commas	Compound words
• Performance poetry	Subject/verb agreement	Dictionary skills
• Features of non-fiction	Notes	Proof-reading for spelling errors
• Instructions	Punctuation; Correct sentences	Spelling strategies
• Characterisation; Story themes	Key words; Grammatical awareness	Syllables

Writing Focus 2.2   Giving instructions; Plans; Rules; Handy hints for editing your work

• Characterisation	Adjectives	Prefixes
• Fact and fiction; 'Time' words	Personal pronouns – singular and plural	Words within words
• Stories by same author	Pronouns; Subject/verb agreement	Synonyms and homonyms
• Author language; Prediction	Use of 1st and 3rd person	Spelling strategies
• Fact and fiction	Conjunctions; Word order	Syllables

Writing Focus 3.1   Story sequel; Story plans; Writing stories; Making a book; Book reviews; Handy hints for writing stories

• Humorous poetry	Sense and accuracy	Spelling strategies; Phonemes
• Types of letter; Audience	Possessive pronouns	Common expressions
• Locating facts; Alphabetic texts	Conjunctions; Past tenses	Apostrophes; Spelling
• Word puzzles, puns and riddles	Punctuation	Spelling strategies
• Library classification systems	Grammatical sense and accuracy	Spelling strategies

Writing Focus 3.2   Writing Letters; Make a non-fiction book; Handy hints for editing your work

	Poster	Range	Text Level
1.1	The Sandcastle	Story with familiar setting	Settings and characters; Expressing personal views; Story endings; Writing stories; First-person voice
1.2	Shape Poems	Shape poetry	Use of describing words; Layout and presentation; Rhyming; Expressing personal views; Calligrams; Shape poems
1.3	Weather	Poetry based on observation and the sense	Layout and structure of poems; Rhyming; Use of describing words; Comparing poems; Collecting words and phrases
1.4	Going Shopping	Story with familiar setting; Story writing; Playlets	Setting; Characters; Dialogue; Comparing stories; Nouns (including proper and collective nouns); Devices for presenting text; Commas in lists
1.5	Nail Soup	Play	Layout of playscript; Dialogue; Use of different voices; Story language; Character description; Story frames; Writing a play; Recipes
1.6	The Noise in the Night	Story with familiar setting	Settings; Dialogue; Use of different voices; Continuing a story; Opening paragraphs
1.7	Using a Dictionary and a Thesaurus	Dictionaries and thesauruses	Use, features and layouts of dictionaries and thesauruses; Explanatory writing
1.8	Under the Sea	Information text	Fiction/non-fiction; Facts; Text structure; Key words; Taking notes; Non-chronological report
1.9	Inside a Castle	Information text	Page layout and structure; Contents page; Diagrams and labels; Fiction/non-fiction; Facts; Non-chronological report; Main ideas; Advantages and disadvantages; Notes
1.10	The Conjuror	Play	Comparing playscripts and prose; Settings; Characters; Playscripts; Dialogue
2.1	Dreamtime	Myth	Story language; Style and voice; Characters; Key events; Story frames; Planning
2.2	How the Squirrel got its Stripes	Legend	Story language; Themes; Characters; Morals; Comparing stories; Plays; Points of view; Planning
2.3	Foxy Fables	Fables	Comparing stories; Morals; Themes; Story language; Characters; Settings; Writing sequels;
2.4	Little Red Riding Hood	Traditional tale	Features of presentation; Picture story; Characters and stereotyping; Sequels; Playscript
2.5	Poems to Perform	Oral and performance poetry	Features of performance poems; Use of punctuation; Planning; Using poems as models for writing
2.6	Theseus and the Minotaur	Legend	Use of language; Characters; Settings; Themes; Paragraphs; Main points; Flow diagrams; Planning; Writing a myth

Sentence Level	Word Level
Take account of grammar and punctuation while reading; Verbs; Dialogue words; Questions; Speech marks	Phonemes; Adding '-ing' to verbs; '-le' word endings; Synonyms; Using a thesaurus; Dialogue words
Verbs; General punctuation	High frequency words; Letter strings; '-le' word endings; Synonyms; Using thesaurus; Dictionary work
Using grammar and other cues when reading; Verbs; Punctuation – full stops and commas	Verbs ending in '-ing'; Purpose and organisation of dictionaries; Using a dictionary
Reading with attention to punctuation; Verbs – past tense;	Phonemes; Pluralisation; Contractions using apostrophes
Reading with attention to punctuation; Dialogue; Verbs; Adjectives; Speech marks; Commas in lists	Phonemes; Proof-reading; Root words and suffixes; Synonyms; Using a thesaurus
Verbs (synonyms, tenses); Speech marks; Dialogue	Phonemes; High frequency words; Alphabetical order; Synonyms (dialogue words)
Word classes; Nouns; Verbs; Devices for presenting texts; Sentence structure and punctuation	Spelling strategies; Using a dictionary and thesaurus; Synonyms
Verbs – 'doing' and 'being' words; Auxiliary verbs; Exclamation marks	Spelling strategies; Synonyms
Verbs; Adjectives; Subject/verb agreement; General punctuation	Phonemes; Letter strings; Compound words; Silent letters; Plurals; Definitions; Alphabetical order
Taking account of grammar and punctuation while reading; Writing a playscript in prose; Speech marks	Prefixes; Antonyms
Adjectives (functions, alternatives, classification); Proper nouns and capital letters	Compound words; Context cues; Definitions; Using a dictionary
Use of grammar and punctuation while reading; Adjectives; Verbs; Collective nouns; Speech marks; Commas; Singular and plural	Suffixes (verbs ending in '-y', adverbs in '-ly', comparison of adjectives); Spelling strategies; Silent letters; Antonyms; Alphabetical order; Definitions
Singular and plural; Collective nouns; Subject/verb agreement	Silent letters; Comparing adjectives; Alphabetical order (second letter)
Adjectives; Singular and plural; Use of third- and first-person	Contractions using apostrophes; Compound words; Letter strings; High frequency words; Antonyms
Singular and plural; Proper nouns; Classifying adjectives; Verbs; Capital letters in poetry; Commas	Rules for pluralisation; Rhyming words
Adjectives; Commas	Prefixes; Suffixes ('-ful' and '-less'); Alphabetical order; Definitions

	Poster	Range	Text Level
2.7	More Poems to Perform	Oral and performance poetry	Preparing and reading poems; Taking account of punctuation and meaning; Features of poems; Comparing themes; Extending poems; Retaining style and rhythm
2.8	Park Farm	Information leaflet; Instructions	Purpose of instructional texts; Features of text organisation; Evaluating text; Using a plan for writing directions; Making own plan
2.9	How to Make a Pop-up Card	Instructions	Purpose of instructional texts; Features of text organisation; Reading and following instructions; Writing instructions and directions; Sequencing instructions; Flow diagrams
2.10	The Great Flood	Myth	Comparing themes; Story language; Analysing story structure; Note-making; Writing myths
3.1	On the Run	Adventure and mystery story	Use of language for effect; Characters; Settings; First-person narrative; Writing next chapter
3.2	Fantastic Mr Fox	Adventure and mystery story	Use of language for effect; Awareness of authors; Credibility of events; Characters; Writing sequels; Writing a review
3.3	Sophie Meets the BFG	Adventure and mystery story	Use of language for effect; Characters; Awareness of author; Comparison of work by same author; Descriptive writing; Writing a review; Language play; Biographical writing
3.4	Treasure Island	Adventure and mystery story	Awareness of author; Settings; Characters; Writing story modelled on text; Story openings
3.5	Face to Face with a Tiger	Real-life adventure	Text layout and structure; Sequencing; Characters; Credibility of events; Comparison of similar texts; Writing true-life adventure; First-person account
3.6	Poems for Fun	Humorous poetry; Language play	Poems with language play; Poet's use of language; Evaluating appeal of poems; Comparison of similar poems; Writing poems
3.7	Writing Letters	Writing letters for different purposes	Purposes of different types of letter; Tone and formality; Writing letters for different reasons; Notes and messages
3.8	Information Books	Information texts; Alphabetic texts	Fiction/non-fiction; Scanning texts; Features of information books; Contents and indexes; Making an information book
3.9	Playing with Words	Word puzzles, puns and riddles	Comparing forms of humour; Different types of writing with language play
3.10	In the Library	Library skills	Dewey system; Location and classification of books in libraries; Rules; Explanatory texts

Scope and Sequence	
Sentence Level	**Word Level**
Classifying adjectives; Using bold and italics; Capital letters; Pronouns	Contractions using apostrophes; Antonyms
Singular and plural; Capital letters; Second-person	Syllables; Using a dictionary
Verbs; Prepositions; Singular and plural; Collective nouns; Text deletions; Second-person narrative	Suffixes ('-ly', '-ful', '-less'); Prefixes; Compound words; Words spelled the same but with different meanings
Evaluating use of adjectives; Word order in sentences	Comparison of adjectives; Suffixing; Alphabetical order; Using a dictionary
Pronouns; Words and phrases signalling time sequence	Spelling strategies; Letter strings; Using words in different contexts
Pronouns; Gender; Conjunctions and connectives	Prefixes; Homonyms; Words spelled the same with different meanings
Adjectives describing nationalities; Pronouns; Grammatical agreement; Speech and exclamation marks; Conjunctions	Prefixes; Suffixes; Phonemes; Letter strings; Dialogue words; Synonyms; Using a thesaurus and dictionary
First- and third-person narratives; Conjunctions	Syllables; Letter strings; Homonyms; Using a thesaurus and dictionary
First- and third-person; Types of pronouns; Singular and plural; Commas; Conjunctions	Comparing adjectives; Suffixes; Common expressions
Adjectives; Verbs; Pronouns; Punctuation in poems; Speech marks	Phonemes; Rhyming; Alliteration; Contractions; Silent letters; Words spelled same but with different meanings; Common expressions
Pronouns; Punctuating letters; Conjunctions	Suffixes; Syllables; Spelling strategies; Common expressions
Nouns; Verbs; Features of texts	Root words and suffixes; Syllables; Classification of words by theme
Pronouns; General punctuation	Contractions; Silent letters; Homonyms
Persuasive use of words – nouns, verbs and adjectives; Use of capitals in book titles	Letter strings; Word origins

Weekly Planner for the Literacy Hour

(Using Letts Poster Packs, Literacy Activity Books, Differentiated Activity Books for Sentence and Word Level)

Week beginning:

	Class	Year Group(s)		Term	Teacher	Plenary
	Whole class – shared reading and writing	Whole class – phonics, spelling, vocabulary and grammar	Guided group tasks (reading or writing)	Guided group tasks (reading or writing)	Independent group tasks	
Mon						
Tues						
Wed						
Thur						
Fri						

Termly Planner for the Literacy Hour

Term

(Using Letts Poster Packs, Literacy Activity Books,
Differentiated Activity Books for Sentence and Word Level)

Class	Year Group(s)	Teacher

	WEEK NUMBER			
Text Level	**Sentence Level**	**Word Level**	**Texts: Titles and Range**	
1				
2				
3				
4				
5				
6				
7				
8				
9				
10				

The Sandcastle

About the poster

This extract is taken from one of a series of books written by Magdalen Nabb about the everyday experiences and life of a girl called Josie Smith.

Teaching opportunities at:

TEXT Level
Reading comprehension

1 Look at the title, picture, introduction and the text to identify the setting of the story. What can be discovered? *(The setting is a holiday at the seaside. There are many clues to support this.)* Ask the children to use their imagination and previous experience to add other details about the seaside, e.g. what might be seen, smelled or heard.

2 *a)* Use the text to explore the characters, their behaviour, relationships and feelings. Who features in the story? How old are they? What is their position in the family? *(The story is about Gran (the two girls' grandmother), Josie, and Josie's sister Eileen. The age of the characters will depend on the children's interpretation.)*

b) How is Josie kind to her sister? *(Josie has spent all her money on a windmill for her sister.)* What was the effect of this? *(Josie had no money left.)* What did Josie really want? *(She wanted to buy some flags for her sandcastle.)* How did Josie feel when she saw all the flags on other people's sandcastles? How can you tell? *(She felt she was missing out and didn't want to play anymore. She was upset.)*

c) Why is Gran on the beach with Josie? What does Josie's Gran look like? Where might Mum be? *(Answers will depend on*

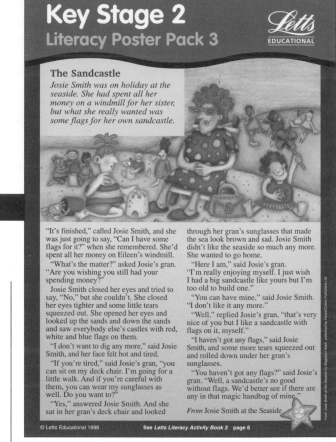

Key Stage 2
Literacy Poster Pack 3
Letts EDUCATIONAL

The Sandcastle
Josie Smith was on holiday at the seaside. She had spent all her money on a windmill for her sister, but what she really wanted was some flags for her own sandcastle.

"It's finished," called Josie Smith, and she was just going to say, "Can I have some flags for it?" when she remembered. She'd spent all her money on Eileen's windmill.

"What's the matter?" asked Josie's gran. "Are you wishing you still had your spending money?"

Josie Smith closed her eyes and tried to say, "No," but she couldn't. She closed her eyes tighter and some little tears squeezed out. She opened her eyes and looked up the sands and down the sands and saw everybody else's castles with red, white and blue flags on them.

"I don't want to dig any more," said Josie Smith, and her face felt hot and tired.

"If you're tired," said Josie's gran, "you can sit on my deck chair. I'm going for a little walk. And if you're careful with them, you can wear my sunglasses as well. Do you want to?"

"Yes," answered Josie Smith. And she sat in her gran's deck chair and looked through her gran's sunglasses that made the sea look brown and sad. Josie Smith didn't like the seaside so much any more. She wanted to go home.

"Here I am," said Josie's gran. "I'm really enjoying myself. I just wish I had a big sandcastle like yours but I'm too old to build one."

"You can have mine," said Josie Smith. "I don't like it any more."

"Well," replied Josie's gran, "that's very nice of you but I like a sandcastle with flags on it, myself."

"I haven't got any flags," said Josie Smith, and some more tears squeezed out and rolled down under her gran's sunglasses.

"You haven't got any flags?" said Josie's gran. "Well, a sandcastle's no good without flags. We'd better see if there are any in that magic handbag of mine."

From Josie Smith at the Seaside.

© Letts Educational 1998   **See** *Letts Literacy Activity Book 3*   **page 6**

the children's interpretation.) In what ways is Gran thoughtful and kind? *(She let Josie sit on her chair and wear her sunglasses.)* What surprise did she have for Josie? *(She bought some flags and hid them in her handbag.)*

3 Discuss how the text is laid out. Talk about the importance of the title. *(It encompasses the central theme of the story.)* Note that the introduction is in italics. Why? What purpose does it serve? *(It differentiates it from the main text and acts as a summary.)* Notice how dialogue is set out, i.e. starting a new line each time someone speaks, and that speech is demarcated by speech marks.

4 Who wrote the passage? *(The author is Magdalen Nabb, as credited at the bottom of the page.)* Find some other 'Josie Smith' books by Magdalen Nabb. Read them with the children and make comparisons.

Writing composition

1 Write descriptions of known settings familiar to the children, such as the seaside or the park, including the characters from the passage.

2 Ask the children to continue the story in their own words. Encourage them to include dialogue, laying it out in the same way as the dialogue in the extract.

3 Discuss how the story could be written from Josie's point of view – in the first-person. Consider how it would be written down. For example, 'I told Gran I'd finished'.

4 Ask the children to record their opinion of the story in the form of a book review. They should include the title, the author and what they liked or disliked about it.

SENTENCE Level
Grammatical awareness

1 Discuss the variety of 'dialogue' words used, in place of 'said', to describe the way in which things were spoken. ('Called', 'asked', 'answered' and 'replied'.) Think of some other 'dialogue' words that could be used.

2 Focus on the function and use of verbs in the passage. Describe them as 'doing' words. Read some sentences and identify the verbs. (Answers will depend on the section chosen.) Note how two words are sometimes used to represent verbs, for example, 'was playing'. Try changing the verbs or substituting other verbs. Try saying the sentences with the verb left out. How does this affect the meaning?

Related texts:

Other titles by Magdalen Nabb:
'Josie Smith and Eileen'
'Josie Smith at Christmas'
'Josie Smith at School'
'Josie Smith at the Market'

Sentence construction and punctuation

1 Find some examples of questions in the text. How can they be identified?

2 Ask the children to make up their own questions about the text and to punctuate them correctly.

3 Find some examples of dialogue in the text. Ask the children each to read the words spoken by one character only. Discuss the fact that only spoken words go inside the speech marks. Note the configuration of speech marks and the fact that the first word spoken always begins with a capital letter.

WORD Level
Spelling

1 Undertake 'phoneme' or 'letter pattern' hunts in the text. Look for words containing specific phonemes or letter patterns, e.g. 'ai', 'ck', etc. ('Said', 'deck'.) Introduce other words, with the same letter patterns, to add to the list,
e.g. 's<u>ai</u>d', 'm<u>ai</u>d', 'cont<u>ai</u>n';
'd<u>eck</u>', 'p<u>eck</u>', 'wr<u>eck</u>', 'ch<u>eck</u>', etc.

2 Use some of the verbs in the text to consider what happens to the root words when the suffixes '-ing' or '-ed' are added. (For example, 'wish' becomes 'wishing' and 'wished'; 'like' becomes 'liking' and 'liked'; 'cry' becomes 'crying' and 'cried'; 'hug' becomes 'hugging' and 'hugged'.)

Vocabulary extension

1 Encourage the children to use a thesaurus to look up synonyms (words with similar meanings) for words in the text, such as 'finish' (end) and 'remember' (recall).

2 As a class, list as many 'dialogue' verbs, 'movement' verbs and 'eating' verbs as possible. Again, the children might use a thesaurus for help.

Shape Poems

About the text

This poster consists of a number of shape poems based around a range of themes.

Teaching opportunities at:

TEXT Level
Reading comprehension

1 The best starting point is simply to spend time reading and enjoying these poems. You can both read them to the children and allow the children to read them on their own or in pairs or groups. Encourage the children to use different expressions and voice tones, using their voices to capture the spirit and sounds of the poems. Accompany the poems with actions, where appropriate.

2 Discuss the different uses of language: the strong descriptive words like 'streaks' and 'sizzles'; the alliterative element in the 'slithery snakes slide'; the use of rhyming in the snowman; and the action verbs for the frog, like 'hop' and 'jump'.

3 Consider the way the poems are presented and set out. Note how the pictures and shapes are used to contextualise the poems and add meaning. Discuss how the title 'Lightning' captures the concept. Ask for suggestions why these are called 'shape' poems. *(The layout of the poems mirror the words visually.)* How are the words of the snake and frog poems set out? *(The snake is set out in a wiggly line and the frog is set out as bouncing words.)* Do the children think this adds to the poems? Point out the way the snowman and fire poems are incorporated into the pictures of a snowman and a fire.

4 Consider whether all the poems rhyme. Discuss whether a poem has to rhyme or not. What makes the non-rhyming poems effective?

5 Encourage the children to express their opinions and views on the poems. Which did they like? Which did they dislike? Why?

Writing composition

1 Choose single words like 'pop!', 'shout', 'snow', 'fire', 'tall', 'mountain', etc., and play with them on the board, asking the children for suggestions on how the lettering can be presented in different ways to make a calligram (a word picture). This could then be extended to whole phrases or sentences, such as about a worm wriggling, or snail sliding, which could be written inside the shape of the thing being described.

SENTENCE Level
Grammatical awareness

1 Notice the powerful use of verbs in the poems. Identify all the verbs and write them on the board. *(Lightning: 'streaks', 'flashes', 'sizzles', 'crashes'; Snakes: 'slide', 'making', 'hissing'; Snowman: 'make', 'stop'; Fire: 'snap', 'leap', 'blaze', 'hiss', 'roar', 'spark', 'fizz', 'crackle'; Frog: 'hop', 'jump'.)* Use the Lightning poem, in particular, to highlight the function of verbs in sentences.

Sentence construction and punctuation

1 Note how the letters are different sizes and shapes. Note, too, that only capital letters are used in the poems. Discuss whether this matters or not.

WORD Level
Spelling

1 There are many common high frequency and interesting letter patterns in the poems, for example, 'ea', 'ou', 'ow'. *('ea': 'streaks', 'leap'; 'ou': 'ground', 'sound'; 'ow': 'snowman'.)* These could be looked for and used as a basis for generalising other words by analogy, for example, by matching common letter patterns.

2 Use the words 'bobble', 'crackle' and 'sizzles' to focus on the '-le' at the end of words. Ask for further suggestions from the children. *(They may point out 'while' and 'smile' from the poems.)* Ask the children to find other words in their books ending in '-le'.

Vocabulary extension

1 Use a thesaurus to look up synonyms (words with a similar meaning) for some of the interesting words in the poems. Try substituting some of the words found. *(For example, 'slither' might become 'skitter', 'slide' or 'skate'.)* Does it make a difference? Does it improve the poems?

2 Use a dictionary to check the meaning of words the children do not know in the poems.

Related texts:

'A Red Poetry Paintbox' chosen by John Foster (collection)

'A Blue Poetry Paintbox' chosen by John Foster (collection)

'Balloon' by Colleen Thibadeau from 'First Poems' compiled by Julia Eccleshane (a delightful shape poem)

'Out for the Count' by Kathryn Cane (a 'Counting Adventure')

'Scrumdiddly' compiled by Jennifer Curry (a wonderful collection of poems, many of which are non-rhyming)

'My First has Gone Bonkers' by Brian Moses (a highly recommended book which includes shape, number, play with words, fun poems, picture poems, etc.)

'A Diddle-Duddle Day' by Joan Poulson (from 'Twinkle Twinkle Chocolate Bar' compiled by John Foster)

'Fancy Me' by Janet Paisley (also from 'Twinkle Twinkle Chocolate Bar')

'A Big Bare Bear' by Robert Heidbreder (also from 'Twinkle Twinkle Chocolate Bar')

NB The last three poems are alliterative.

Weather

About the text

What can be a more familiar topic of everyday conversation than the weather? This poem takes a look at weather throughout the year, and is arranged chronologically in months.

Teaching opportunities at:

TEXT Level
Reading comprehension

1 Read the poem to the children and discuss the way it is set out. How many verses does it have? *(It has 12 verses.)* How many lines are there in each verse? *(There are two lines.)* What is special about each verse? *(Each verse is about one month.)* What is the theme of the poem? *(Characteristics of each month.)*

2 Draw attention to the fact that the poem is rhyming. Ask the children to find the rhyming words. *('Beginning/spinning'; 'fogs/ logs'; 'spring/sing'; 'slow/grow'; 'pole/foal'; 'in/skin'; 'out/drought'; 'holiday/stay'; 'come/ one'; 'trees/seas'; 'cold/old'; 'light/bright'.)*

3 There are some good examples of alliteration to show the children, for example, 'February frosty fogs'. There are also some good descriptive words that could be used for class discussion, for example, 'gales lash the trees' and 'brave blackbirds', etc. Can the children think up their own alliterative sentences?

4 The poem could be practised and performed. Suggest it is done in pairs, with each child reading alternate lines. Alternatively, it could be done in verses, with different children reading particular verses.

5 There are many 'weather' poems in anthologies, such as 'Wind' by Jean Kenward, 'Winter Walk' by Wendy Larmont, 'Weather'

Key Stage 2
Literacy Poster Pack 3
Letts EDUCATIONAL

Weather

January new beginning,
Resolutions, snowflakes spinning.

February frosty fogs,
Winter shivers, fire-warm logs.

March blows windy, smells of spring,
Leaves peek out, brave blackbirds sing.

April showers fall soft and slow,
Earth wakes up, and green things grow.

May Day ribbons round a pole,
May-time babies, lamb and foal.

June brings summer blazing in,
Scent of roses, sun on skin.

July joy means school is out,
Time for picnics, heat and drought.

August goes on holiday,
Sandy castles, friends to stay.

September sees the autumn come,
Plough the fields, one by one.

October gales lash the trees,
Leaves a-swirling, crashing seas.

November nights all crisp and cold,
Winter coats for young and old.

December dark, yet full of light,
Christmas carols, stars so bright.

Lucy Coates

© Letts Educational 1998   See *Letts Literacy Activity Book 3*   page 10

by Theresa Heine and 'The Summer Sun' by Wes Magee. Find other examples and compare and contrast them.

Writing composition

1 The structure of the poem lends itself well as a framework for writing similar poems – perhaps as a class discussion or after-class activity. Brainstorm and list ideas, phrases and expressions on the board for each month, or ask individual groups to choose a month each and pool their ideas.

2 The same structural approach could be taken for writing a poem about 'My Week'.

SENTENCE Level
Grammatical awareness

1 Encourage the children to use their awareness of grammar, along with other cues, to decipher new or unfamiliar words in the poem.

2 With the class, compose one complete sentence about each month, underline the verb in each full sentence and discuss its function, e.g. 'In January it often <u>snows</u>'. *(The underlined verbs will depend on the children's full sentences.)*

Sentence construction and punctuation

1 When reading the poem aloud, focus on the importance of punctuation for giving meaning, and, in particular, the use of full stops and commas.

WORD Level
Spelling

1 There are lots of verbs ending with '-ing' in the poem. *('Beginning', 'spinning', 'blazing', 'swirling' and 'crashing'.)* Select a variety and note what happens when this suffix is added to the root verb, for example, 'crash' becomes 'crashing'; 'blaze' becomes 'blazing'; 'spin' becomes 'spinning'. Generate some rules and think of other examples for each rule. *(Most verbs: simply add '-ing'; verbs with a short vowel sound plus consonant: double the consonant and add '-ing'; verbs ending with a silent 'e': drop the 'e' and add '-ing'.)* Find some other '-ing' verbs in reading books. Decide what the root verb is for each example.

Vocabulary extension

1 Use a dictionary to look up a word which is unfamiliar to the children, such as 'drought'. In so doing, reinforce the purpose and organisation of dictionaries. *(Point out the key word at the top corner of each page and the alphabetical order.)*

Related texts:

'A Year Full of Poems' by Michael Harrison and Christopher Stuart-Clark (a really excellent book with poems for every season and weather condition!)

'The Puffin Book of Twentieth Century Verse' edited by Brian Patten

Going Shopping

About the poster

This is a story about a boy called Chips. The story is told in picture frames (like a comic) with the dialogue in speech bubbles. It is one of a series of Chips stories, written by Shirley Hughes.

Teaching opportunities at:

TEXT Level

Reading comprehension

1 Discuss the setting for the story. What clues are there in the title, the pictures and the text as to the setting? *(There are many clues that it is set in a supermarket – the shop sign, the shopping list, the trolley, the aisles of food, etc.)*

2 Who are the characters in the story? *(Mum, Chips, Chips' sister, Gloria, Chips' friend, Jessie and Jessie's dog, Burkis.)* How do we know their names? *(They are all spoken at some point.)* What can we tell about each character from the story? *(Answers will depend on the children's interpretation.)* How much attention is the mother paying to Chips and how much to her shopping list? *(Mum is paying far more attention to the shopping than to Chips.)* How does Chips behave in the supermarket? *(He runs about.)* Who is the little girl? *(She is Jessie, owner of the dog which is tied up outside.)* Is she on her own? *(We don't know.)* Can the dog be considered as a character? *(Yes, he has thought bubbles.)* What can we tell about the dog? *(He is bored and resentful at being left outside.)* Can dogs really think? How do they express themselves? *(Answers will depend on the children's interpretation.)* How can you tell the baby is only young? *(The baby is small and rides in a buggy and in the seat of the shopping trolley. She is carried, doesn't talk properly yet, isn't involved in any conversations, etc.)*

3 Discuss how the text is laid out. *(It is a sequence of pictures, with dialogue in speech bubbles.)* How is this different from conventional stories? *(Stories are usually continuous text with the speech in speech marks.)* What can be noticed about the dog's 'speech'? *(It is a thought bubble rather than actual speech.)* What can be noticed about the baby's speech? *(The baby speaks in 'baby' language rather than proper words.)*

4 Notice the use of exclamation marks and the situations in which they are used. *(For emphasis.)* Notice how capital letters are also used for emphasis.

5 Invite the children to relate the story to their own experiences of shopping. Allow anecdotes about likes and dislikes, and things that have happened whilst shopping.

Writing composition

1 Ask the children to continue the story in pictures, with dialogue in speech bubbles. Use the text as a model.

2 The story could be rewritten as a short play, and acted or read out in small groups, with different children reading the parts.

3 As a class, brainstorm other adventures Chips could have. Plan the ideas and translate them into story form using storyboards, telling the story in a sequence of pictures. This, too, could be used to write a playscript.

SENTENCE Level
Grammatical awareness

1 Use some of the verbs from the passage to talk about present and past tenses. Retell the story as if it is happening in the present and then as if it happened yesterday. For example, 'Chips is going to the supermarket' and 'Yesterday Chips went to the supermarket'.

2 The supermarket theme provides a good opportunity to discuss nouns, i.e. names of people, places and things. Children could look at the pictures and name the things they can find. (*They might point out 'cheese', 'eggs', 'supermarket', 'dog', etc. There are many other nouns.*) Mention that names of people are special nouns and should begin with capital letters. (*Chips, Jessie, Barkis and Gloria.*)

Sentence construction and punctuation

1 Draw pictures of characters in different situations and use speech bubbles, e.g. a motorist stopping to ask someone for directions. Ask the children to write in the bubbles what they think each character is saying. Ask the children to write a short sentence about each picture and to punctuate it correctly.

2 Draw the children's attention to the use of commas in Mum's shopping list. ('*... cheese, eggs, tomatoes, biscuits, washing powder, cereal...*') Children could then make up their own shopping lists, using commas to separate the items.

WORD Level
Spelling

1 Find some examples of common phonemes in the text, e.g. 'ee', 'ea', 'ar', 'ow', 'oo', 'ie', 'igh', 'ie'. (*For example, 'ch__ee__se', 'l__ea__ve', 'B__ar__kis', 'p__ow__der', 'g__oo__d', 't__oo__', 't__ie__', 't__igh__t', 'fr__ie__nd'.*) Use them as a basis for drawing up lists of other words containing the same phonemes and generating spelling activities. Use a dictionary to check the definitions.

2 Use the text as a starting point for investigating the rules for the pluralisation of nouns. Point out 'egg' becomes 'eggs', 'buggy' becomes 'buggies', 'dish' becomes 'dishes' and 'shelf' becomes 'shelves', etc. (*Most nouns: simply add 's'; nouns ending in a consonant plus 'y': change the 'y' to 'i' and add 'es'; nouns ending with 'sh', 'ch', 'x' or 'ss': add 'es'; nouns ending in 'f': change the 'f' to 'v' and add 'es'.*)

3 There are several examples of contractions using an apostrophe in the text, such as 'can't', 'we'll' and 'I'm'. Examine and discuss them as a class.

Vocabulary extension

1 Study the antonyms (opposites) of words, using examples from the text as starters. (*'Inside/outside' and 'good/bad' are two examples.*)

2 Ask the children to suggest definitions for some of the objects in the extract, like 'buggy' and 'trolley'. Dictionaries could be used to help.

Related texts:

Shirley Hughes has written many books in the 'Alfie' series, all of which are worth reading.

Nail Soup

About the poster

This is a retelling in play form of an old, traditional story.

Teaching opportunities at:

TEXT Level
Reading comprehension

1 Discuss the layout of the text, noting the way dialogue is represented, identifying the different characters and explaining the role of the narrator. *(Dialogue has no speech marks and is always preceded by the name of the character who is speaking. There are three characters – the Narrator, the Old lady and the Man. The narrator 'describes' what is going on.)* Ask the children to suggest how the passage is different from continuous prose. *(The story is told in the dialogue of the characters and narrator. Putting text into parts to be spoken is a distinctive way to structure the text.)*

2 What clues in the text and illustration tell us that the story is set in the past? *(The kitchen and characters' clothes are very old-fashioned, and the story begins 'Once upon a time...')* Where is the story set? *(It is set in a village.)*

3 Which words could be used to describe the man? How did he behave towards the old lady? Ask the children for their opinion of the beggar. *(Answers will depend on the children's interpretation.)*

4 Describe the old lady's appearance from the illustration. Was she kind or foolish? *(Answers will depend on the children's interpretation.)*

5 In what way is this a tale of trickery and cunning? Is there a moral to the story?

Key Stage 2
Literacy Poster Pack 3
Letts EDUCATIONAL

Nail Soup

Narrator: Once upon a time there was a poor beggar. He had no money and was always hungry. One day as he was walking through a village he saw a nail on the ground. As he bent down to pick it up he had an idea.

Old lady: Good morning. What's that you've got there?

Man: It's a nail for making soup. If you let me come in I'll show you.

Narrator: So the old lady took the man into her house and gave him a pan and some water. The man put the nail into the pan and began to boil up the water. He took a deep sniff.

Man: This is going to be the best soup ever! Have you got such a thing as a carrot? It needs a bit of colour.

Narrator: The old lady gave him the carrot and he put it in the soup. The man stirred it and sniffed it again.

Man: Can I have an onion? That would help give it more flavour.

Narrator: The man chuckled slyly to himself.

Man: All it needs now is a chicken and some salt and pepper to finish it off.

Narrator: The old lady hurried off and got the things the beggar asked for. The smell was delicious. A little later the soup was ready to serve.

Man: Shall we have some nice, fresh, crispy, crusty bread to go with it?

Old lady: Of course. I'll just get some.

Narrator: When she returned they sat down and ate the soup.

Old lady: This is marvellous! I wish I had a nail like yours for making soup.

Man: They are not easy to come by, you know. But as you've been so kind to me, you can have mine as a special gift.

Narrator: The old lady held the nail tightly as she waved goodbye to the man. The man whistled happily to himself and smiled.

© Letts Educational 1998   See *Letts Literacy Activity Book 3* page 14

6 Which words at the beginning alert the reader to the fact that it is going to be a particular type of story? *('Once upon a time...')*

Writing composition

1 The children could retell the story in a series of picture frames with simple captions and speech bubbles. Remind the children of the layout of 'Going Shopping' (page 12).

2 The story could be retold in the first-person from either the old lady's, or the beggar's, point of view. Does this change the 'tone' of the play? How does it affect the listeners' sympathies to the characters?

3 Write a sequel to the play in which the beggar tries the trick on another person, but this time, he himself is outwitted.

SENTENCE Level
Grammatical awareness

1 Read the play in groups, asking different children to take on the parts of the various characters. Encourage them to take account of the punctuation and to read with expression.

2 Write out, or ask the children to copy, some of the Narrator's dialogue. Ask the children to identify the verbs and underline them. *(Answers will depend on the passage chosen.)* Try substituting other verbs with similar meanings. What, if any, difference do they make?

3 Use the same text again and experiment with deleting words to see how the meaning is affected. For example, if the pronouns are missed from this sentence, it makes quite a difference: 'The man stirred _____ and sniffed _____ again.'

4 Use the passage to work on adjectives, e.g. 'nice, fresh, crispy, crusty bread'. Discuss the difference they make to meaning.

Sentence construction and punctuation

1 Write out the passage, or part of the passage, for the children as a story text, punctuated correctly and including speech marks. Leave out the dialogue in the speech marks, but leave space for children to write in the words, as a way of focusing on dialogue.

2 Ask the children to list the ingredients of the soup, using commas to separate the items. *(Water, a nail, a carrot, an onion, a chicken, some salt and pepper.)* Extend this to other lists, e.g. eating implements, kitchen utensils, etc.

WORD Level
Spelling

1 Look for words in the passage that contain the phonemes 'ai', 'ay', 'ou', 'ow', 'oo', 'or', 'er', 'oi', 'ee'. ('N<u>ai</u>l', 'alw<u>ay</u>s', 's<u>ou</u>p', 'n<u>ow</u>', 'g<u>oo</u>dbye', 'p<u>oor</u>', 'th<u>er</u>e', 'b<u>oi</u>l', 'd<u>ee</u>p', etc.) Use the words for word-building and to generate other words containing the same phonemes.

2 Rewrite a section of the text, but include some misspellings. Show it to the children. Ask them to read the text and to try to spot the mistakes. Encourage them to check the new passage against the original and compare. Have they missed any errors?

3 Look at the words 'crispy' and 'crusty'. Ask the children which shorter words they have come from. *('Crisp' and 'crust'.)* Try adding the suffix '-y' to other nouns to turn them into adjectives and see what effect, if any, it has on the spelling of the root word, e.g. 'sun' becomes 'sunny' and 'hunger' becomes 'hungry'.

4 Find some examples of adverbs ending in '-ly' in the text. *(Point out 'slyly', 'tightly' and 'happily'.)* Provide the children with some more adjectives to which they can add '-ly' and discuss any changes there might be, for example, 'slow' becomes 'slowly' and 'easy' becomes 'easily'.

Vocabulary extension

1 Use a thesaurus to find synonyms (words with a similar meaning) for words from the text, like 'nice', 'sniff', 'wave', 'easy', etc.

Related texts:

'Cinderella', 'Beauty and the Beast' and 'Aladdin' by Terri Wiltshire (from the 'Children's Fairytale Theatre)

'Little Red Riding Hood' by Moira Butterfield

The Noise in the Night

About the text

This extract from Philippa Pearce's 'The Battle of Bubble and Squeak' is when Mr and Mrs Sparrow are awoken by a strange sound in the middle of the night...

Key Stage 2
Literacy Poster Pack 3

Letts EDUCATIONAL

The Noise in the Night

The middle of the night, and everyone in the house asleep. Everyone? Then what was that noise? Creak! and then, after a pause, Creak! And then, Creak!...

Mrs Sparrow heard it. The noise woke her, as the crying of her children would have woken her. But this was someone else's job. She nudged her husband. She nudged and nudged until Bill Sparrow stirred, groaned. He had been dreaming of the garden.

"Bill!" she whispered. "Come on! Wake up!"

"Yes," he said. "Just a minute, and I'll do that."

"Listen."

Creak! and then, Creak! And then, Creak!

"Can't you hear it?"

"Yes."

"What is it?"

"I don't know."

"But it's in the house!"

"Yes, it is."

"Downstairs!"

"Yes."

"Bill, what are you going to do about it?"

He nearly said again, "I don't know." Then he pulled himself together. He tried to think clearly what he ought to do. First he

ought to wake up properly. Then, he ought to get up. He ought to find out what was making that noise that bothered Alice so. That was it: find out.

"I'm getting up," he said out aloud. "I'm going to find out about that row downstairs."

He reached for the pencil torch that Mrs Sparrow kept under her pillow. He wouldn't switch on the lights; he wouldn't even use the torch until he had to. He would surprise whatever it was. Whoever it was.

From The Battle of Bubble and Squeak by Philippa Pearce

© Letts Educational 1998

See *Letts Literacy Activity Book 3* page 20

Teaching opportunities at:

TEXT Level
Reading comprehension

1 Before reading the story, look at the title and the picture and ask for suggestions predicting what the passage might be about, and what the setting for the story is likely to be. *(Answers will depend on the children's interpretation.)*

2 Discuss how, at night-time, noises seem to be louder, or take on a different significance. Discuss why this might be. Children, if allowed, will recount many anecdotal experiences!

3 When reading the story, draw attention to the way much of it is in the form of dialogue. How is this indicated? *(There are speech marks.)* Note that each time a new person speaks a new line is begun. Encourage an awareness of the different 'voices' in the passage.

4 Find and discuss examples of statements, questions and exclamations in the dialogue in the extract. How are they different? *(Statements end with a full stop, questions end with a question mark and exclamations end with an exclamation mark.)*

5 If possible, have a copy of the book from which the passage is taken available for children to read if they wish.

Writing composition

1 How do the children think the story will continue? Try writing the next section of the story, incorporating dialogue in it as far as possible. Use the extract as a model.

2 The setting of the story is good for stimulating ideas for children's own personal writing. Why not use the same title or the same opening paragraph for a new story? Ask the children to jot down lots of ideas before choosing the best and drafting it. Can the draft be revised and improved?

SENTENCE Level
Grammatical awareness

1 Brainstorm verbs connected with sleeping, for example, 'sleeping', 'dozing', 'dreaming', 'stirring', 'turning over', 'snoring', 'waking', etc. Ask the children to write some sentences using the new words.

2 Using the theme of the story, focus on past tenses, especially irregular ones, e.g. 'I hear' becomes 'I heard'; 'I see' becomes 'I saw'; 'I go' becomes 'I went'; 'I catch' becomes 'I caught', etc. Encourage the children to rewrite some of the passage in the present tense.

Sentence construction and punctuation

1 Discuss the basic conventions of speech punctuation. Identify speech marks and note how capital letters are always used at the start of direct speech. Point out that punctuation always appears inside the speech marks, too.

2 Encourage the children to suggest other things Mr and Mrs Sparrow might say and to record these in writing, either on the board as a class exercise or individually.

WORD Level
Spelling

1 Write a number of common spelling patterns on the board, such as 'ee', 'ar', 'oi', 'ow', 'ou', (revising Year 2 spelling patterns). Hold a wordsearch competition to see who can find any examples in the passage. *(These include 'asleep', 'garden', ' noise', 'downstairs', 'ought', etc.)*

2 The same approach may be used for spotting high frequency words, using the High frequency word list (see page 74) as a starting point.

Vocabulary extension

1 Encourage the children to write down five words they find interesting from the passage. Ask them to write them in alphabetical order and to make up definitions for them. Then ask the children to look up the meanings in a dictionary and correct any they had wrong.

2 Think up some more 'dialogue' words to use instead of 'said' in the text. *(The text uses 'whispered'.)* Brainstorm and list as many others as possible.

Related texts:

'Who's Afraid and Other Strange Stories' by Philippa Pearce

'A Century of Children's Ghost Stories: Tales of Dread and Delight' by Philippa Pearce (NB These would be most suitable for Y3 fluent readers.)

'The Day Matt Sold Great Grandma' by Eleanor Allen and Jane Cope

'Clive and the Missing Finger' by Sarah Garland

'Jimmy Woods and the Big Bad Wolf' by Mick Gowar and Barry Wilkinson

Using a Dictionary and a Thesaurus

About the text

The poster comprises of a section from a dictionary and one from a thesaurus, identifying the key features of each.

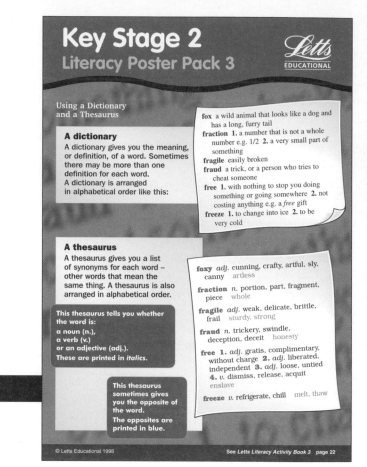

Teaching opportunities at:

TEXT Level
Reading comprehension

1 Use the poster to consolidate knowledge of dictionaries and thesauruses, to develop skills in using them and to introduce new ideas and concepts relating to them. Use the poster alongside class dictionaries and thesauruses to compare and contrast, and then practise lessons learned. *(Cover issues such as alphabetical order, more than one meaning, key words, whether words are nouns, adjectives or verbs, etc.)*

2 Focus on the fact that both books are arranged in alphabetical order, and ensure that the children understand what 'alphabetical order' means.

3 Discuss the different functions of each book. *(A dictionary gives meaning and a thesaurus gives a list of synonyms.)* Introduce and discuss the terms 'definition' and 'synonym'. *(A definition is what something means and a synonym is a word with a similar meaning.)*

Writing composition

1 Ask the children to explain, in their own words, the purpose of each type of book and their main features.

2 Help the children to write their own, small dictionary containing their favourite words. Then make sure they check the words in a dictionary to ensure they follow alphabetical order and have the correct meaning.

SENTENCE Level
Grammatical awareness

1 Notice that the thesaurus on the poster identifies words according to their class, e.g. noun, verb and adjective. Discuss the fact that words have different functions in sentences, and review the function of nouns and verbs within the context of simple sentences. *(Nouns describe objects or things and verbs describe actions.)*

2 Practise organising sets of nouns or verbs in alphabetical order.

Sentence construction and punctuation

1 Discuss the way information is structured, presented and laid out in the dictionary and thesaurus extracts. *(Include the use of bold to pick out the words, the italics to describe the class of the word, the lesser bold to show the antonym (opposite).)*

2 Lead on from Writing Composition, question 2, and ask the children to practise writing out simple definitions of words, using proper sentences and punctuating them correctly.

WORD Level
Spelling

1 Choose some of the tricky words from the poster, like 'fraud'. Write them on the board. Discuss the difficult parts of each word, then try to think of other words with similar letter patterns. After studying and discussing the words for some time, cover them and encourage the children to try and write them from memory. Check their attempts against the originals. Ask them to identify any mistakes by referring to the originals, and repeating the activity. Discuss the importance of looking very carefully and trying to 'photograph' the image of words in the mind. Remind the children of the 'Look, say, cover, write, check' method.

Vocabulary extension

1 Hold dictionary and thesaurus 'races'. Ask the children to practise finding specific words in their own books.

2 Use thesauruses to find, classify and use synonyms (words with similar meanings). Discuss the meanings of the synonyms, or shades of meaning. Can the children spell the words without looking?

Related texts:

All classrooms are equipped with both of these text books and many teachers keep to their own particular favourites. One very useful volume is the Brimax 'Junior Illustrated Dictionary', but there are many very good 'First Dictionaries'.

Under the Sea

About the text

This poster is a fairly typical non-fiction, factual text from an information book. It is structured in paragraphs about different underwater sea creatures.

Teaching opportunities at:

TEXT Level
Reading comprehension

1 Look at the title and background illustration on the poster. Ask the children to suggest what they think the poster might be about.

2 Ask whether they think the text will be a fiction or non-fiction text, explaining their reasons. *(Make sure the children realise that it is non-fiction.)* Ensure the children understand the difference between the terms 'fiction' and 'non-fiction'. Use the term 'fact' in the explanation.

3 Ask the children to notice how the text is structured, i.e. in six paragraphs, with each paragraph about a different aspect of life under the sea.

4 Read the 'Did you know…' introduction. Consider its role as a 'lead-in' or 'warm-up' to the main theme. *(It intrigues and draws the reader in.)*

5 Read each paragraph to and with the children. Ask them to suggest in one or two words what the main topic of each paragraph is. *(For example, plankton – Blue Whales – dolphins – octopuses – sharks – plants.)*

6 Ask specific factual questions about each paragraph to encourage literal comprehension, e.g. 'Why are people afraid of sharks?'

Writing composition

1 As a class, encourage the children to offer two or three key points about each paragraph. Write the key words only on the board to demonstrate the skill of note-making. At the end, reflect on how brief notes provide a skeleton of the main text.

2 If appropriate, use another reference book on the same topic of the sea. Ask the children to look for further information and facts on the aspects covered in the extract. Integrate these into the notes already made.

3 Encourage the children to write a simple, factual text using information already known, structured along the same lines as the text studied. Use titles like, 'On the Farm' or 'In the Woods'. Ask the children to work in pairs or small groups to pool their knowledge and to write three or four different paragraphs on the different aspects of life there.

SENTENCE Level
Grammatical awareness

1 Identify the verbs in each sentence. Reread the sentences, leaving out the verbs, and note the difference this makes to the meaning. *(There are many possible examples.)*

2 Verbs are often described as 'doing' words, for example, plants 'grow'. There are several examples of 'being' verbs in the text, too. Find them and make up some more sentences, using 'being' verbs. *(For example, 'Whales are…', 'Dolphins are…'.)*

3 Verbs often need a small 'helper', or auxiliary verb, e.g. dolphins 'can talk' and 'the Blue Whale can grow'. Look for such verbs in the text and in other reading books and make a list.

Sentence construction and punctuation

1 Notice how the exclamation mark is used in the text to indicate surprise. *(Paragraph 2: 'as much as 200 small cars!')* Encourage the children to inflect their voices appropriately when reading exclamations. Find some more examples of exclamations that demonstrate surprise, shock, noise, etc., in other texts.

WORD Level
Spelling

1 Ask the children to identify several tricky words in the text and list them on the board, for example, 'plankton'. Study the words and ask the children to suggest things that could help them to remember their spellings. *(Underline the unusual parts of the word. Look for small words within larger words. Look for common spelling patterns and think of other similar words. Break the word down into parts.)* Practise the 'Look, say, cover, write, check' method on the words.

Vocabulary extension

1 Ask the children to suggest synonyms (words with similar meanings) for some of the words in the text, e.g. 'small', 'talk', 'afraid', 'fierce', 'strong', 'grow', etc. *(There are many possible answers.)* Make a class list for future reference and use.

Related texts:

'Monsters of the Deep' by Saviour Pirotta

'Seals' by Michael Bright

'Big Blue Whale' by Nicola Davies

'The Blue Whale' by Melissa Kim

'Whales and Dolphins' by Steve Parker

'Sharks' by Amanda Harman

Inside a Castle

About the poster

This is an explanatory text about the features of a castle, presented in diagrammatic form with caption labels. The contents page of the book from which it came is incorporated to help place the page in the context of the book as a whole.

Teaching opportunities at:

TEXT Level
Reading comprehension

1 Discuss the layout of the page. Ask what the importance of the title and introduction are. (*They summarise what the book is about.*) What is a contents page? (*It describes what is in the book.*) Which section of the book would this page have come from? (*From 'Inside a castle', page 8.*) Discuss how the diagram is cut away and how the use of arrowed labels, combined with the picture, provide essential information.

2 Ask the children to articulate what the purpose of the page is. (*It explains the rooms and their function in the castle.*)

3 Discuss whether this is taken from a fiction or non-fiction book? How is it possible to tell this? (*It is non-fiction. Point out that there is no dialogue and consider the type of language used; it contains many facts; the text is not written in continuous prose.*)

4 Encourage the children to look for key information and to record what they think the ten most important facts on the page are. (*There are many possible answers.*) They should write in note form rather than in full.

5 Ask the children to give each label a heading as a way of encouraging them to grasp the main idea of each section. This should be one or two words only, if possible.

6 Ask questions based on the contents page, to familiarise the children with its usage, e.g. 'Where was food kept?'.

Writing composition

1 Ask the children to make up and write their own label for the spiral stairs. Remind them to supply a heading.

2 Encourage the children to use the information provided on the page to write a report about what they have learned about castles.

3 Divide a page into half, lengthways, and label one column 'advantages' and the other column 'disadvantages'. After class discussion, ask the children to list what the pros and cons of living in a castle might be. *(Answers will depend on the children's interpretation. Which wins?)*

4 Children could imagine they were the lord or lady of the castle. What sort of things might they do? Brainstorm what a 'day in their life' might be like. Write notes on the board. Then ask the children to write their own version in prose based on the notes.

SENTENCE Level
Grammatical awareness

1 Identify the verbs in the labels. *(There are many to choose from.)* Draw attention to the fact that most of them consist of two words, e.g. 'was drawn'. How do the children think this aids meaning and clarity?

2 Ask the children to describe particular areas of the castle, using lots of adjectives, e.g. 'The hall was a large room containing long tables. It was heated by a roaring fire in winter'. Make sure that the adjectives are appropriate to the context.

3 Supply the children with some statements about the castle in which the subject and verb disagree. Ask the children to spot the mistakes and correct them, e.g. 'The lord sleep in a four-poster bed,' or 'The supplies was kept in the store room'.

Sentence construction and punctuation

1 Ask the children to write some questions of their own, based on the text, and to punctuate them correctly. Check any tricky words in a dictionary.

WORD Level
Spelling

1 Provide the children with some common phonemes and letter strings and ask them to find words in the text which include them, e.g. 'aw', 'er', 'ie', 'oo', etc. *(Some examples are 'dr<u>aw</u>n', 'w<u>a</u>ter', 'enem<u>ie</u>s', 'bedr<u>oo</u>ms', etc.)*

2 Use the compound words from the text – 'drawbridge', 'bedrooms', 'everyday' – as a starting point for thinking of other compound words and listing them. Can the children separate the words into the constituent parts?

3 Use the compound words, or other multi-syllabic words, to consider how breaking a word into syllables might help with spelling, e.g. 'en/ter/tain/ing'. Supply a list of multi-syllabic words for the children to divide up.

4 Two words from the text – 'ghost' and 'castle' – both contain silent letters. Explain what these are and provide the children with other examples to look at and say, in order to identify the silent letters in them. *(Silent letters are not heard when the word is spoken, in this case 'h', 't' and 'e'.)* Use a dictionary to find some words beginning with 'wr' and 'kn'. Can the children spot the silent letter?

Vocabulary extension

1 Ask the children to write definitions for some of the words on the poster. Encourage them to use a dictionary for help. Then write the words in alphabetical order.

2 Take several words from the text which begin with the same letter, e.g. 'window', 'water', 'well', etc., and ask the children to place them in alphabetical order, according to the second letter. *(In this case, 'water', 'well', 'window'.)*

Related texts:

'Forts and Castles' by Brian Williams

'The Best Ever Book of Castles' by Philip Steele

'Castle' by Christopher Gravett

'How Castles Were Built' by Peter Hicks

'A Medieval Castle' by Fiona Macdonald

'Royal Castle – The Inside Story' by John Farndon

'The Story of the Castle' by Miriam Moss

The Conjuror

About the text

Most children will have attended parties at which a conjuror has been hired for the entertainment.

This passage is taken from a playscript on this theme.

Teaching opportunities at:

TEXT Level
Reading comprehension

1 Discuss the way the text is laid out. How is it possible to tell it is a playscript? *(Dialogue has no speech marks and is always preceded by the name of the character who is speaking. There are also stage directions in italics.)* How are the different characters' parts signified? *(By their names.)*

2 Read the passage to and with the children. Consider how the setting is made clear. *(Through the illustration, the storyline and the stage instructions, etc.)*

3 Discuss the various characters in the story and the way they behave. Discuss, in particular, Stuart! *(The children all enjoy the show and take part. Stuart is determined not to be impressed and acts as the 'heckler'. Your children will add greatly to this.)*

4 Consider the conjuror's name and ensure children 'get' the pun (play on words).

Writing composition

1 Ask the children to consider how the play might continue. As a class, continue the play together, reinforcing points learned about dialogue, setting, etc.

2 Talk about parties together. This could stimulate many possible writing activities. Ask the children to list the food and drink they would have (ensuring that the lists are correctly punctuated with commas). Ask them to design a party menu or invitation. Ask them to write a thank you letter for a present received and to design a birthday card of their own.

SENTENCE Level
Grammatical awareness

1 When reading aloud, encourage the children to take the grammar and punctuation of the passage into account, e.g. the use of commas, question marks, exclamation marks, etc. Discuss how these affect the way the words are spoken.

2 Discuss the jobs people do, e.g. a conjuror performs tricks, a teacher teaches, a musician plays music, etc. Give the children a list of people and ask them write what each one does. Use this to stress the function of verbs as 'doing' words.

Sentence construction and punctuation

1 Notice, in particular, the way dialogue is represented in playscripts. Practise rewriting some of the dialogue, but this time using speech marks to reinforce work done previously.

WORD Level
Spelling

1 The theme of conjurors is very good for introducing prefixes by using words like 'disappear', 'reappear', etc. Discuss the effect they have on the meaning of words and also on their spelling. Brainstorm words that can be prefixed by 'un-', 'dis-', 'de-', 're-' and 'pre-'.

2 The theme is also good for 'disappearing' letter patterns. Choose a pair of phonemes or letter patterns which you wish the children to study. Provide them with a number of words but with the chosen letter patterns missing, e.g. 'm_ _ l' for 'meal'. The children then decide which letter pattern is missing and rewrite the words correctly. (You might like to provide cryptic clues for the words to help.)

Vocabulary extension

1 Use the work on prefixes to focus on antonyms (opposites). Extend it generally to thinking of opposites with, or without, prefixes, for example, big and small; happy and unhappy, etc.

Related texts:

Here are some suggestions for riddles and jokes material which could be used for inclusion in children's own playlets, etc.

'The Funniest Riddle Book in the World' by Morrie Gallant

'Duck for Cover' by Paul Jennings

Plays from the 'All Aboard' and 'New Reading 360' Reading Programmes from Ginn

'The Ozone Friendly Biodegradable Creepy Crawly Joke Book' by Teresa Green

'Rhymes and Riddles' by Fran Pickering

'Take Part' series of plays (adapted by Lane and Kemp) ideal for mixed ability groups

'What am I? Very First Riddles' by Stephanie Caimenson (excellent for Y3 more reluctant readers.)

Dreamtime

About the text

This is a retelling of the traditional Australian creation story, told by the Aborigines.

Teaching opportunities at:

TEXT Level
Reading comprehension

1 Discuss the fact that there are many stories, passed down from generation to generation and in various cultures, which try to explain how the world began. These are called 'creation stories'. Ask the children to suggest why they are so called. Why do people all over the world tell these stories? (*Answers will depend on the children's interpretation.*)

2 Read the story aloud, pointing out examples of language typically used to structure such types of stories. (*'At the beginning', 'after a while', etc.*) Collect examples from other stories. Ask the children to suggest common ways to introduce and conclude such stories, for example, 'A long time ago…' and '…and they lived happily ever after'.

3 Identify the main characters of the story. Ask the children to describe them – their appearance, behaviour, things they said, etc. (*The main characters are the Rainbow Serpent and the big-bellied frogs. Their descriptions will depend on the children's interpretation.*)

Writing composition

1 As a class, discuss the key events in the story. Write them on the board in note form, linking them with arrows. (*The Rainbow Serpent awakes → she comes to the surface → she sees the big-bellied frogs → she tickles their tummies → the frogs laugh → water gushes out of them → the land grows green.*) Consider how each of these events could be represented as a separate storyboard, or picture frame, telling the story.

2 Brainstorm how the story might continue, using the same technique. Ask the children to write their own version or draw storyboards with captions.

3 Use the earlier discussion on characters as a way of doing some character portraits, for example, a paragraph on each, as a poster or as a labelled diagram, etc.

SENTENCE Level
Grammatical awareness

1 Reread the passage, this time omitting all the adjectives. Discuss what difference this makes. Consider the function adjectives serve. *(To dramatise, to enliven and to make more descriptive, etc.)*

2 Experiment with substituting alternative adjectives and discuss what difference this makes. Make a class list of alternative adjectives for later reference.

3 Is it possible to classify the adjectives in the passage according to colour, size, mood and so on? *(For example, 'huge' and 'fat' are to do with size.)* This will engender lots of discussion on how adjectives are used.

Sentence construction and punctuation

1 The name of the Rainbow Serpent begins with capital letters. Use this as a way of focusing on proper nouns – special names of people, places and things. Ask the children for words that begin with capitals. *(There are many possible suggestions and most children will start with their own names.)* Examine them and discuss the reasons.

WORD Level
Spelling

1 The word 'rainbow' is a compound word, consisting of two separate, shorter words. *('Rain' and 'bow'.)* Find other examples of compound words in the passage, for example, 'dreamtime', 'everything', 'inside', 'someone', etc. Ask the children to suggest some more compound words and make a class list. Then provide the children with word sums, e.g. butter + fly = _____ and ask them to work out the answers. Encourage them to make up their own word sums to try out on each other.

Vocabulary extension

1 Ask the children to try and define, in their own words, the meanings of some of the more difficult words in the text, using the context of the word to help them, e.g. 'snigger', etc. Then ask the children to look the words up in a dictionary, compare them and refine their definitions. Can they also write them in alphabetical order?

> ### Related texts:
>
> 'The Creation of the World' by Claude and Catherine Ragache
>
> 'How the World Began and Other Stories of Creation' by Andrew Matthews

How the Squirrel got its Stripes

About the poster

This is just one of the many Indian legends about Rama and Sita.

Teaching opportunities at:

TEXT Level
Reading comprehension

1 Explain that a legend is a traditional story about heroic characters, which may have some element of truth, but which has been embellished over the years. Note how there are clues in the language that this is an old story. (*'Long ago'*, *'to this very day'*.) This legend is built around the important figures of Rama and Sita and their story. There are really two stories running side by side – the story of Rama's battle with Ravana and an explanation of how the squirrel got its stripes.

2 Discuss whether animals really speak. What does this tell us about the type of story this is? (*Animals can't really speak so it contains elements of fantasy.*)

3 How did the monkeys treat the squirrel? Why? (*They jeered and were cruel because they thought she was too small to help.*)

4 Ask the children to consider the squirrel's feelings at different parts in the story.

5 What can be learned about Rama's character from the story? (*He is wise and kind.*)

6 Ask the children to suggest a moral for the story.

7 Find and read different Rama and Sita stories, and other animal stories explaining how they got certain physical characteristics (The 'Just So Stories' by Rudyard Kipling are a very good example). Compare and evaluate them.

Key Stage 2
Literacy Poster Pack 3

Letts EDUCATIONAL

How the Squirrel got its Stripes

Long ago in India Lord Rama lived with his beautiful wife, Sita. Nearby on the island of Sri Lanka lived Rawana, a wicked Demon King. One day Rawana kidnapped Sita and carried her off to his island. Lord Rama asked the monkeys to help him build a bridge to the island and rescue his wife.

The monkeys worked very hard. They carried piles of rocks every day to build the bridge. Suddenly, one monkey noticed a small squirrel who was also helping.

"What are you trying to do?" he laughed.

"I'm helping Rama to build his bridge," the squirrel replied.

"But you are too small to help," smiled the monkey.

"No, I'm not," answered the squirrel. "I can bring little pebbles."

Then all the other monkeys began to laugh and told the squirrel not to be so silly. They told her to go back home and leave the work to them.

But the little squirrel took no notice and just carried on as before. One monkey got angry, grabbed hold of her tail and threw her out of the way. She went flying into the air but when she came down Lord Rama caught her. He had overheard everything.

He held the squirrel gently and called all the monkeys to gather round. He told the monkeys that they should not have behaved in such a way.

"Even weak, tiny creatures can show their love, and can serve in different ways," he said. Then he stooped down and put the squirrel on the ground. "Little one," he said softly, "you have loved and served me well." Then he stroked the squirrel on her back and left his finger marks for all to see.

Still, to this very day, the Indian squirrel has three white stripes on its back where it was once stroked by Lord Rama.

An Indian legend

© Letts Educational 1998   See *Letts Literacy Activity Book 3* page 36

Writing composition

1 Describe the squirrel's character. (*For example, patient, unassuming, helpful, etc.*)

2 The story could be rewritten as a playscript as there is a good deal of dialogue in it. Remind children of the layout of a playscript by revisiting 'The Conjuror', page 24.

3 Ask the children to tell the story from the squirrel's point of view. This can be in the first person if they prefer.

SENTENCE Level
Grammatical awareness

1 When reading the story aloud, encourage the children to take proper note of the grammar and punctuation marks. (*Speech marks, commas, question marks, full stops, etc.*)

2 Look for adjectives in the passage and discuss the purpose they serve. This could lead onto a class discussion, classifying adjectives that describe size, colour, feelings, etc. (*There are many possible examples.*)

3 Use the passage to point out that verbs may be either 'doing' ('the monkeys <u>worked</u> very hard') or 'being' ('you <u>are</u> too small') words. Ask the children to find further examples in the text. (*There are many possible answers.*)

4 The monkeys carried 'piles of rocks'. Use this example to talk about collective nouns and to think of other examples, such as 'a gaggle of geese'.

Sentence construction and punctuation

1 Draw attention to the use of speech marks in the passage and the punctuation conventions associated with them. (*The first word of a new sentence starts with a capital letter, and the final punctuation – commas, full stops, etc., comes within the closing speech marks.*)

2 Find some examples of singular and plural nouns in the passage. (*There are many examples: 'the monkeys', 'the squirrel', 'pebbles', 'bridge', etc.*) Examine how singular nouns may be pluralised. (*Make sure the children are aware that it is not always effected simply by adding an 's'.*) Discuss what effect this has on spelling. (*For example, adding an 's', adding 'ies', etc.*) Consider, too, what changes occur in sentences when singular nouns are changed into the plural, in terms of subject/verb agreement.

WORD Level
Spelling

1 Explain that a suffix is a letter or group of letters added to the end of words, to change their meaning in some way. Note how the spelling of the past tense of verbs in the passage ending in consonant + 'y' are affected. For example, 'carry' becomes 'carried', 'reply' becomes 'replied'. Find examples of adverbs ending in '-ly' in the text and discuss what the root of each word is. (*Suddenly, gently, softly – sudden, gentle, soft.*) Think of some other adverbs and do the same.

2 Use some of the adjectives from the text to explore their comparative forms. (*'Small, smaller, smallest'; 'angry, angrier, angriest'; 'gentle, gentler, gentlest'.*)

3 Look for words in the text containing silent letters and discuss their spelling. (*There are many examples, e.g. 'island', 'build', 'bridge', 'rescue', 'answer', etc.*) Which letters are silent? Are they always vowels? Make a list and discuss.

Vocabulary extension

1 Think of words opposite in meaning to some of the adjectives in the text and write them in two columns.

2 Look for words in the text beginning with the same letter. (*build, bridge, back*) Ask the children to order them alphabetically according to their second letter. (*back, bridge, build.*)

3 Ask the children to write out their own definitions for some of the words in the story, e.g. 'island', 'bridge', 'kidnap'. Then check the words in a dictionary.

Related texts:

'How Rabbit Stole the Fire: A Folk Tale from North America' by Joanna Troughton

'Just So Stories' by Rudyard Kipling

'Realms of Gold: Myths and Legends from Around the World' by Ann Pilling

'The Orchard Book of Stories from the Seven Seas' retold by Pomme Clayton

Foxy Fables

About the text

The poster shows two short fables about foxes by Aesop.

Key Stage 2
Literacy Poster Pack 3

Letts EDUCATIONAL

Foxy Fables

The Greedy Fox

One day a clever fox saw a shepherd putting his dinner inside a hollow tree before setting out to look after his flock of sheep. When the shepherd was out of sight the fox ran over to the tree. The gap in the trunk was very narrow, but by pulling in his sides the fox managed to squeeze inside.

Once he was in the tree, the fox gobbled up the food until every bit was gone. Then he tried to get out of the tree again. To his horror he found that he had eaten so much that his stomach had grown plump. No matter how hard he tried he could not squeeze back out again. Now when the fox realised he was trapped he began to howl. One of his friends, who was passing by, came to see what the matter was. "There's nothing I can do," he said. "You'll just have to wait until you grow thin enough to get out again. I hope the shepherd doesn't return before then!"

The greedy fox was annoyed with himself for being so silly.

Moral: We should think before we act.

The Crafty Fox

One day a crow was sitting on a branch of a tree holding a piece of cheese in her beak. She was just getting ready to eat the cheese when a hungry fox looked up and saw her. The fox put on his best smile and said, "Hello Mrs Crow. How lovely you look today." The crow was very pleased and nodded her head but said nothing.

"Oh my! I bet you are a beautiful singer. I am so tired I would like to rest under your tree. Can you sing me to sleep?"

Now when the crow heard the fox's praise she was very flattered. As she began to sing she let go of the cheese and it fell to the ground. The fox immediately jumped on it and gobbled it up. He smiled up at the crow and politely said, "Thank you!" The hungry crow was annoyed with herself for being so silly.

Moral: Beware of flattery. It may not be meant.

Aesop's Fables

© Letts Educational 1998

See *Letts Literacy Activity Book 3* page 38

Teaching opportunities at:

TEXT Level
Reading comprehension

1 Before introducing the text, explain that a fable is a story with a moral, i.e. it tries to teach us a lesson of some sort.

2 Read the two stories and discuss them. Consider and discuss the character of the fox in each of the stories. Consider, too, the character of the crow. (*Answers will depend on the children's interpretation.*)

3 Identify the theme of each story. (*Think before you act, and beware of flattery – it is not always meant.*)

4 Does the moral fit each story? (*It does.*)

5 Examine some of the common language of traditional stories like these, for example, the way each story begins and ends. You might like to look again at 'Dreamtime', page 26, for ideas.

6 Find and read other fables particularly those by Aesop. Ask the children to suggest an appropriate moral for each of them.

7 Biblical parables are also good to read as stories with a moral or lesson.

Writing composition

1 Encourage the children to write character portraits of the foxes and the crow from the stories.

2 Think of and write other stories to illustrate the same morals – using the same characters; changing the characters; changing the settings, etc. Compare the children's stories and discuss their ideas.

3 Provide the children with some other words, e.g. 'more haste, less speed' and ask them to make up their own fables to illustrate them.

SENTENCE Level
Grammatical awareness

1 Select examples of nouns from the passage and use them to discuss singulars and plurals. *(There are many possible examples.)* Present the words in the singular and then pluralise them. Discuss what changes are necessary to the spelling. *(Ensure the children appreciate it is not always effected by simply adding 's'.)*

2 In the passage, find the collective noun 'flock of sheep'. Ask the children to list other examples they know, such as 'a herd of cattle', 'a pile of stones', etc.

Sentence construction and punctuation

1 Choose a few sentences from the text and rewrite them, ensuring that the verb and subject do not agree, such as 'The gap in the trunk were very narrow...', 'I bet you is a beautiful singer...'. Ask the children to identify what is wrong with each sentence and explain why.

WORD Level
Spelling

1 Find the word 'shepherd' in the text. Draw attention to the fact that, in some words, certain letters are not pronounced – they are 'silent letters'. Give examples of some of the more common silent letters, e.g. 'b' in 'lamb', 'k' in 'knee', 'w' in 'wrist'. Ask the children to suggest others and make a class list.

2 Talk about comparative and superlative adjectives. Look at the word 'plump'. After the fox had eaten he was 'plumper'. This can be further changed by the addition of the suffix '-est'. Provide a selection of adjectives that can be suffixed by '-er' and '-est' and ask the children to write them, so 'plump' becomes 'plumper' and 'plumpest'. Ensure a variety of words are provided including examples like 'fat' ('fatter', 'fattest'); 'wide' ('wider', 'widest') and 'silly' ('sillier', 'silliest'). Discuss what happens to the spellings in these different cases.

Vocabulary extension

1 Find some words in the passage beginning with different letters for the children to practise arranging alphabetically. Then find some words beginning with the same letter, e.g. 'f', for the children to practise arranging according to their second letter.

Related texts:

'Aesop's Fables' translated by S A Hanford

'The Amazing Talking Pig and Other Stories' by Mick Gower (very funny modern fables)

'Anno's Aesop: A Book of Fables by Aesop and Mr. Fox' by Mitsuma Anno

'Foxy Fables' by Tony Ross (a picture/storybook which is ideal for reluctant readers at Y3)

Little Red Riding Hood

About the text

This traditional story is told as a series of picture frames (like a comic) and captions, and includes dialogue in speech bubbles.

Teaching opportunities at:

TEXT Level
Reading comprehension

1 Discuss the way the story is presented. How is this different from the way most stories are written? *(It is written as a comic strip.)* Ask the children's opinion about the style of presentation. How is speech represented? *(It is in speech bubbles.)* Do they like the illustrations? Do they help make the story clearer?

2 There is a saying that 'a picture saves a thousand words'. What do the children think this means?

3 Ask the children to empathise with the characters. Discuss how each one might feel and what they might be thinking at particular points through the story.

4 The characters in the story all fit fairly rigid stereotypes. Discuss the way in which each is portrayed. *(Scared girl, little old lady, brave woodcutter.)* How might the story be changed to break away from these stereotypes?

Writing composition

1 You might give the story a new twist by asking the children to think of some different ways to finish the story.

2 The story could be rewritten as a playscript. (See 'The Conjuror', page 24, for layout.) Suggest the children try this, and practise reading and performing their plays, including all their different endings.

SENTENCE Level
Grammatical awareness

1 One by one, study each of the characters and list any adjectives that could be used to describe them. *(Answers will depend on the children's interpretation.)* Do the same for the settings in the story too. *(Answers will depend on the children's interpretation.)*

2 Identify the nouns in the passage. *(There are many possible answers.)* Decide whether each is singular or plural. Try pluralising the singular nouns and see what happens. *(Remember, it is not always simply effected by adding 's'.)*

Sentence construction and punctuation

1 Retell the story in the first-person, as if you (the storyteller) were Little Red Riding Hood, e.g., 'One day, I went to see my grandmother.' Discuss with the children any differences this makes to the construction of each sentence.

2 An interesting twist is to try to tell the story, in the first-person, from the point of view of the wolf. Look at the differences this makes to sentence construction.

WORD Level
Spelling

1 Find some words in the text that have been contracted, using apostrophes. *('I'm', 'you've', and 'I'll'.)* Discuss the function of the apostrophe and which letter/s have been omitted. *('I am', 'you have', 'I will'.)* Look for other examples in reading books and write both the contracted and longer forms for each.

2 Find some examples of compound words in the text. *('Grandmother', 'woodcutter' and 'shortcut'.)* Help the children to split words into their correct components.

3 Hold a letter pattern hunt. Provide the children with common letter patterns, like 'ea', 'oi', etc., and ask them to find examples of words in the text containing them, e.g. 'n<u>ea</u>rer' and 'p<u>oi</u>nted'.

4 Hold high frequency word hunts in the same way.

Vocabulary extension

1 Provide the children with a selection of suitable adjectives or verbs from the passage and ask them to supply a word opposite in meaning, e.g., 'wicked' would be 'good', etc.

Related texts:

Walt Disney have produced many old favourites in comic strip format, such as:

'Pinnochio'

'101 Dalmatians'

'Jungle Book'

'Beauty and the Beast'

The books are published by Ravette Publishing.

Poems to Perform
About the poster

The three poems on this poster are all ideal for choral speaking and performance. One is in the 'counting poem' genre. 'Down in the park' has endless possibilities for extension. 'I met a Horse as I went walking' has in-built repetition, telling the story of a journey. (The actual full-length poem does have an ending, although only an extract is included on the poster.) Each poem provides an opportunity for children to make up their own endings.

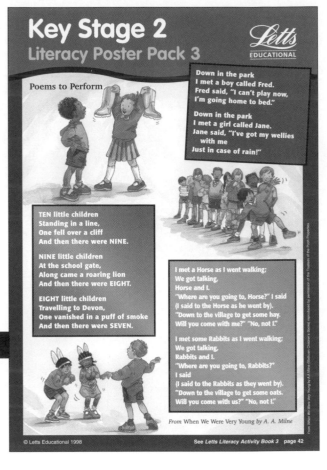

Teaching opportunities at:

TEXT Level
Reading comprehension

1 These poems are great fun to perform and present. They can be read by the whole class, by groups taking different verses, or by pairs of children working together. One successful way of using them is to give groups time to discuss and practise reading them, before attempting a 'public' performance. Draw their attention to the possible ways of dividing up the reading, for example, by verse; by different people reading different parts of the dialogue, etc. Encourage the children to identify suitable expression, tone, volume and use of voices and other sounds, where appropriate.

2 Discuss the features of each poem with the class. Use terms like 'verse', rhyme', 'rhythm'. Talk about each of these aspects. *(Elicit the fact that each poem has an element of predictability and repetition.)* How is this helpful? How is it effective? *(For example, verses help to structure the poems' rhyme and also help to reinforce the structure and predictable nature of the poems. Rhythm helps with the 'feel' and helps when 'performing' the poems.)*

3 When reading the poems to the class initially, draw their attention to the punctuation and comment on how important it is to take it into account. Note how the commas, question marks and exclamation marks affect the reading. Draw attention to the use of capitalisation for effect and emphasis.

4 Try to find the ending of the 'I met a Horse as I went walking' poem in a poetry book (it is taken from 'When We Were Very Young' by A. A. Milne). Ask the children how they think it might end, and where they think the writer is going. Do they like or dislike the true ending?

Writing composition

1 Brainstorm ways to extend each poem, one at a time. Jot ideas in rough on the board or on paper. Ask the children to write their own endings. Encourage them to use the same format and features, i.e. verses, rhyme, rhythm and predictability.

2 Try to find other A. A. Milne poems to read and compare, and to copy in to neat.

3 Encourage the children both to find other number poems and to make up their own.

SENTENCE Level
Grammatical awareness

1 Identify the nouns in each poem. *(There are many possible examples.)* Discuss whether they are singular or plural. Point out that the names of particular people and places begin with a capital letter, and are called proper nouns.

2 Find the adjectives and discuss how they tell us more about each noun they describe. *('Little', 'roaring', 'school'.)* It is interesting to note the use of the word 'school' as an adjective in 'school gate'.

3 Find all the verbs in each poem. *(There are many examples.)* Try reading the poems and missing out the verbs. Remind children that every sentence must contain a verb. Can they guess the missing word?

Sentence construction and punctuation

1 Discuss the different uses of capital letters in the poems. *(The start of a line, proper nouns, names, emphasis and personal pronouns.)*

2 Discuss how commas are used in the poems and what job they do. *(They add a pause in a line and appear before some speech.)*

WORD Level
Spelling

1 Work out the plural version of each singular noun in each poem. Discuss how the spelling of nouns changes. *(They are not always pluralised simply by adding an 's'.)* Note that nouns like 'rain', 'oats', 'smoke' and 'hay' can't be pluralised.

2 Focus on the rhyming words. Which of them sound the same and have the same letter strings or phonemes? *('Fred/bed', 'line/nine', 'walking/talking'.)* Which have different letter strings or phonemes? *('Jane/rain', 'gate/eight', 'Devon/seven', 'I/by'.)* Think of some more words for each set of rhyming words.

Related texts:

Other A. A. Milne favourites include:

'Christopher Robin Verse Book'

'The Hums of Pooh: Lyrics by Pooh'

'Pooh's ABC'

'Stories of Winnie the Pooh Together with Favourite Poems'

'Now We are Six'

Theseus and the Minotaur

About the text

This poster is a simple retelling of the ancient Greek legend.

Teaching opportunities at:

TEXT Level
Reading comprehension

1 Before reading the story, explain that a legend is a traditional story about heroic characters which may, possibly, be based on some element of truth, and which has been passed on through generations. In so doing, legends have been added to and embellished over the years.

2 Read the story. Ask the children to identify words, phrases or expressions used to conjure up the chilling atmosphere of the passage. *(There are many possible answers.)*

3 What sort of person was Theseus? Was he brave? Was he foolish? What thoughts and feelings would have been rushing through his head in the labyrinth? *(Answers will depend on the children's interpretation.)*

4 How does the writer describe the Minotaur? What sort of creature was it? *('It was two metres tall and was half human and half animal. Its head was like a shaggy bull with curved horns as sharp as razors. Its eyes flashed fire. From the neck downwards it was human and had a huge, hairy, barrel chest'.)*

5 What problems did Theseus face? How did he overcome them? *(He faced a maze but took a ball of wool to unravel as he went. He also faced the Minotaur!)*

6 Ask the children to talk about any other stories they have read in which the hero wins against overwhelming odds, such as 'The Seven Labours of Hercules'.

Key Stage 2
Literacy Poster Pack 3

Letts
EDUCATIONAL

Theseus and the Minotaur

King Minos of Crete was protected by a fearsome monster called the Minotaur. It was two metres tall and was half human and half animal. Its head was like a shaggy bull with curved horns as sharp as razors. Its eyes flashed fire. From the neck downwards it was human and had a huge, hairy, barrel chest. The Minotaur did not eat ordinary food. It fed on human flesh!

Now the Minotaur was so savage and dangerous that King Minos kept it hidden in a dark, dank maze of caves and tunnels called the Labyrinth. Each year Minos sent seven boys and seven girls down into the Labyrinth. They were never ever seen again. The people of Crete were terrified that King Minos would choose their children to feed to the Minotaur.

In the end, Princess Ariadne, the daughter of King Minos, took pity on the people. She persuaded Theseus, a young warrior, to climb down into the Labyrinth and get rid of the Minotaur for ever. Ariadne told him to take a ball of wool and unwind it as he passed through the maze of tunnels so that he could find his way out again afterwards.

With trembling legs, Theseus began to grope his way through the pitch-dark twisting tunnels. In a short while Theseus heard the snuffling of the monster as it smelt him coming. A blood-chilling roar echoed through the passages as the Minotaur charged. Theseus knew he could never defeat the monster face to face so he decided to trick it. He flattened himself against the cave wall as

the beast thundered towards him. Its foul stink filled his nostrils and the ground beneath his feet shook as the monster thundered past him. It passed so close to him that its bristly hair scratched his chest like thorn twigs.

As soon as it had passed him, Theseus struck the Minotaur with his sword. The monster fell in a heap bellowing with fury but Theseus plunged his sword in again and killed the beast.

He threaded his way back to the surface again and was greeted by cheering crowds. The evil king's protector, the Minotaur, was gone for good. They would never be troubled by it again and all their children could sleep safely in their beds once more.

An ancient Greek legend

© Letts Educational 1998 See *Letts Literacy Activity Book 3* page 48

Writing composition

1 Notice how the passage is divided into paragraphs. Read each paragraph again, one at a time, and decide what it is mainly about. List the important points in note form as a flow diagram, showing the bones of the story and how they link together. *(Description of the Minotaur → where the Minotaur lived and what it ate → Theseus is persuaded to go into the Labyrinth → Theseus' trip into the Labyrinth → the killing of the Minotaur → Theseus' return to the surface.)*

2 Ask the children to make up their own story about an existing, or an imagined, superhero who battles against the odds. *(Suggest they need not be male.)* Encourage them to plan the story first in note form. This may best be done in pairs or groups. Encourage the children to experiment with the impact of different adjectives.

SENTENCE Level
Grammatical awareness

1 The passage is full of powerful adjectives. *(There are many possible examples.)* Experiment by reading the story again, omitting some of these or substituting alternatives. Note any differences this makes to the meaning.

Sentence construction and punctuation

1 Note the variety of ways commas are used in the passage, and discuss their functions in these situations to help the reader make sense of the text and read it with greater expression and understanding. *(They are used in lists of characteristics and for dramatic pauses in the sentences.)* Ask the children to try to read the passage without taking note of the commas. Is it possible? How does it sound?

WORD Level
Spelling

1 Draw attention to the word 'unwind' in the text. Discuss the fact that it is made up of a root verb 'wind' + a prefix 'un-'. Discuss how the addition of the prefix gives the verb the opposite meaning. Ask the children for other examples, using the prefix 'un-'. Carry out a similar exercise, using other prefixes like 'dis-', 're-', 'pre-', etc.

2 Explore how the addition of the suffixes '-ful' and '-less' can achieve the same effect, e.g. 'fearful' and 'fearless'. Brainstorm and list other adjectives ending in '-ful' and '-less'.

Vocabulary extension

1 Ask the children to list five or more powerful words from the text. Write these down alphabetically and ask the children to write their own definitions for each word. Then ask them to check the order and definitions in a dictionary.

Related texts:

'Ancient Greece: Myths and Legends' by Abigail Frost

'Ancient Greek Myths and Legends' by Philip Ardagh

'Greek Myths for Young Children' by Marcia Williams

More poems to perform

About the text

Both poems on this poster are ideal for choral speaking and performance. One has a repetitive chorus and the other is a rap poem.

Key Stage 2
Literacy Poster Pack 3

Letts EDUCATIONAL

More poems to perform

Our Family Comes From Around The World

Our family comes
From around the world:
Our hair is straight,
Our hair is curled,
Our eyes are brown,
Our eyes are blue,
Our skins are different
Colours, too.

*Tra la tra la
Tra la tra lee
We're one big happy family!*

We're girls and boys,
We're big and small,
We're young and old,
We're short and tall.
We're everything
That we can be

*Tra la tra la
Tra la tra lee
We're one big happy family!*

Mary Ann Hoberman

Rap Connected

We were born to rap
We were born to dance
We were born to sing
We are Queens and Kings
We were born to live de life dat we luv
We were born to luv de life dat we live,
We were born to twist

We were born to shout
We can keep it in
We can hang it out
We got riddim in us mate

Get infected,
Shout it loud,
We are connected.

An extract from 'Rap Connected', by Benjamin Zephaniah

© Letts Educational 1998   See *Letts Literacy Activity Book 3* page 50

Teaching opportunities at:

TEXT Level
Reading comprehension

1 Read 'Our Family Comes From Around The World'. Discuss its features, noting that it consists of two verses and a chorus in italics, and that it rhymes.

2 Ask the children what the theme of the poem is. *(The theme is how different people are.)*

3 Encourage them to offer their opinions of the poem and to suggest ways in which it could be performed.

4 Children may have heard of rap. Ask them to try and articulate what they think it means. *(A rap is a form of oral poetry which has a very strong rhythm and rapid pace. Raps are often associated with Caribbean and Afro-Caribbean cultures.)* Are there any clues in this rap that this is the case? *(For example, the way some things are expressed, such as 'riddim' and 'de life dat we luv'.)*

5 Do the two poems have anything in common? *(The theme is similar.)*

6 Practise reading the poems aloud, identifying appropriate expression, tone, volume and use of voices and other sounds. This might be accompanied by some form of percussion.

Writing composition

1 Try adding new lines, verses or lyrics to the two poems, retaining style and rhythm. Or, alternatively, ask the children to try to write new poems but using the same style as the two on the poster.

SENTENCE Level
Grammatical awareness

1 The first poem is good for work on adjectives. Make a list of them. *('Straight', 'curled', 'brown', 'blue', 'different', 'big', 'happy', 'small', 'young', 'old', 'short', 'tall'.)* Then try to classify them according to criteria, such as colour adjectives, size, etc. Ask the children to suggest other adjectives for each category.

Sentence construction and punctuation

1 Discuss the way the rap poem is set out, noting the lines in bold and italics and the line in larger print. Ask the children to suggest why they think it might be set out in this way.

2 Draw the children's attention to the use of capital letters in both poems as part of a poetic convention to begin new lines (even though the line might not be the beginning of a new sentence).

3 Try reading the poems and changing the pronouns in each, for instance, instead of 'our' family, make it 'your' or 'my' or 'their' family and see what differences these make throughout.

WORD Level
Spelling

1 Draw attention to the contraction 'we're'. Discuss what the apostrophe stands for and which letter is missed out. *(The apostrophe connects the two words. The words are 'we are' and the missing letter is 'a'.)* Find some examples of other contractions in reading books and write them in both their contracted and longer forms.

Vocabulary extension

1 The pairs of adjectives in the first poem lend themselves nicely to work on opposites. *('Girls' and 'boys'; 'big' and 'small'; 'young' and 'old'; 'short' and 'tall'.)* Suggest the children write their own 'opposites' poems to reinforce this work.

Related texts:

Three super 'rap' works as follows:

'Doin Me Ed In' by David Orme and Martin Glynn (a whole book of rap poems)

Poem called 'Ref Rap' by Bernard Young (from 'Ere We Go' football poems chosen by David Orme)

'Cyril MC' by Mary Hoffman (a story poem in rap)

Park Farm

About the text

This poster serves several different functions. It is primarily an advertisement for Park Farm. It provides basic information and rules, and also provides a plan of its features. There is also a map of its location.

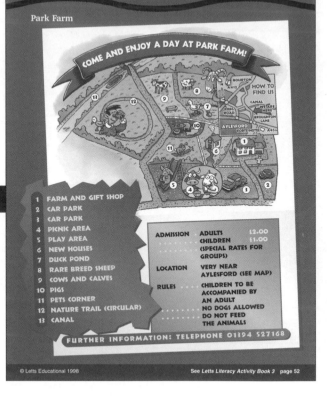

Teaching opportunities at:

TEXT Level
Reading comprehension

1 Look at and discuss the poster. Ask the children how they know what it is about, before studying it thoroughly. *(The title and the picture give you the clues.)*

2 Identify the part of the poster that gives you essential information about cost of admission, etc. *(The table at the bottom.)* Why are rules included? *(For safety and security.)* Where would it be possible to get additional information? *(There is a contact telephone number.)* How clear is this section of the poster? What makes it clear? *(There are many possible answers.)*

3 Why is the 'How to find us' section included on the poster? *(To indicate its position in the country.)* Study this section and discuss its features.

4 How is the plan of the farm different from the 'How to find us' section? *(The plan is a close up.)* How do the pictures and numbers help you to 'read' the plan? *(They provide quick identification without cluttering the picture.)* How does a plan like this help you before you go? *(It makes finding it easy.)* Whilst you are at the farm? *(It is easy to find your way around and see everything.)*

Writing composition

1 Ask the children to describe an imaginary walk about the farm, what they would see, in what order, etc. Encourage them to use appropriate descriptive language when using directions, and words denoting order.

2 Ask the children to explain how they would get from one part of the farm to another, e.g. the route they would take to get from the picnic area to the rare breed sheep.

3 As a class, make up a large poster for an imaginary theme park, incorporating the same features as the plan on the poster. Or you might make a plan of your town or school.

SENTENCE Level
Grammatical awareness

1 Identify the nouns on the poster. *(There are many to choose from.)* Are they singular or plural? If singular, ask the children for the plural, and vice versa. Do they notice that most plurals end in 's'? There are some other interesting nouns to study, for example, 'calf'. Now discuss some other nouns ending in 'f'. Then study words like 'sheep'– nouns that can be singular or plural. Are there other words like this? *(Fish, deer, etc.)* Also discuss the plural 'children' as being unusual.

Sentence construction and punctuation

1 Draw attention to the fact that the poster is printed entirely in capital letters. Why do the children think that is?

2 Point out that the poster is also written in the second-person, although this is never explicitly stated, e.g. 'You' come and enjoy a day at the farm.

WORD Level
Spelling

1 Use the words on the poster as a means to review work on syllables. Decide which are one-, two- and three-syllable words. *(There are many to choose from.)* Write the multisyllabic words and establish where the syllable boundaries are within them. *('En/joy', 'pic/nic', 'hous/es', 'cor/ner', 'na/ture', 'cir/cu/lar', 'can/al', 'ad/miss/ion', 'lo/ca/tion', 'ad/ults', 'child/ren', 'spe/cial', 'Ayles/ford', 'ac/com/pan/ied', 'an/im/als', 'fur/ther', 'in/for/ma/tion', 'tel/e/phone'.)*

Vocabulary extension

1 Use some of the words as opportunities for the children to write and refine definitions, checking their own versions against those given in a dictionary.

Related texts:

'Be Your Own Map Expert' by Barbara Taylor

'Maps and Journeys' by Kate Petty

There are also several guide books to countries for children, such as:

'A First Guide To China' by Kath Davies

How to Make a Pop-up Card

About the poster

This is a straightforward instructional text, giving clear instructions on how to make a simple pop-up card. The text is a combination of written instructions and diagrams.

Teaching opportunities at:

TEXT Level
Reading comprehension

1 Ask the children what sort of a text it is – is it fact or fiction? Is it a story or information text? How can you tell? *(It is a factual, information text. You can tell by the title, the 'What you need' box, the numbered steps, etc.)*

2 What is the purpose of this text? *(To show you how to make a pop-up card.)*

3 Consider, with the children, some of the features of the text – the title; the clear statement of what is needed at the beginning, with bullet-pointed list; clearly marked and numbered steps; concise and to-the-point captions and accompanying diagrams.

4 How is this type of layout helpful to the reader? Why is it logical to have the list of things needed at the beginning? *(To have everything ready before starting to make the card.)*

5 One way of testing how effective and clear the instructions are is to try them out! Do the children find the instructions easy to follow?

6 Where else would you find written instructions? Find examples and compare them for clarity. *(For example, recipe books, gardening manuals, learning to paint books, etc.)*

7 Technology and craft books are often good sources for instructions on 'How to make' projects. Compare how they are laid out.

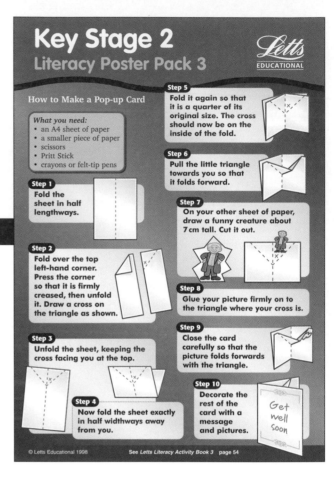

Writing composition

1 Encourage the children to write their own instructions, using the poster as a model to help them structure their writing. Begin by writing about something that the children have actually made recently, perhaps in Technology. Broaden this to more everyday activities such as 'How to make a telephone call', 'How to bathe a dog', etc. This can be further extended to rules for playing games, making recipes, etc.

2 Another possibility is to give children the steps for making something, but in the wrong order. Ask them to rewrite the steps correctly.

3 Writing and giving directions is also closely related. Ask the children to write directions for getting to different places in the school, or to explain the way they get to school.

SENTENCE Level
Grammatical awareness

1 Ask the children to write out some of the steps of the instructions again and underline the verbs. This will help reinforce the idea that verbs are 'doing' words. *(Answers will depend on the section chosen.)*

2 The instructions include many good examples of prepositions, e.g. 'in', 'on', 'inside'. Find them and investigate the function they serve. *(They are positional and clarify instructions.)*

3 Fold a piece of paper lengthways, into two columns. Label the columns 'singular' and 'plural'. Look for the nouns in the text. *(For example, 'paper', 'Pritt Stick', 'crayons', 'pens', 'corner', etc.)* Write them in the appropriate column. Work out and write the missing singular or plural form of each noun. Analyse the nouns. What changes are required to pluralise them? *(Remind the children it is not always effected simply by adding 's'.)* Think of some other examples that follow the same rules.

4 Initiate or continue the work on collective nouns by starting off with the example, 'sheets of paper'.

Sentence construction and punctuation

1 Experiment with the text by deleting certain types of words, e.g. nouns, or verbs, or adjectives, or pronouns, and discussing what difference this makes to the meaning. *(Answers will depend on the section chosen.)*

2 Instructions are usually written in the second-person, although the pronoun 'you' is not included, just assumed. Demonstrate by inserting 'you' in front of the verbs. *(For example, 'You fold the sheet in half lengthways'.)*

WORD Level
Spelling

1 There are two words (adverbs) in the text that end with the suffix '-ly'. Find and write these. *('Firmly', 'carefully'.)* Write out the root word for each and note what changes, if any, are required when the suffix is added. *('Firm+ly', 'careful+ly'.)* Look for other examples in books. Do the same rules apply?

2 Starting with the word 'careful', ask the children to suggest other words that end in '-ful'. Write them on the board. Discuss which root word each comes from. How many of the root words could take the suffix '-less' as well? What effect does this have on the meaning, e.g. careful – careless? *(It makes it the opposite.)*

3 Starting with the word 'unfold' from the extract, brainstorm and write down as many other words that begin with the prefix 'un-'. What is the root word of each? What effect does adding the prefix 'un-' have to the meaning? *(It makes it the opposite.)*

4 Find the compound words in the text and talk about how they are formed. *('Length/ways' and 'in/side'.)*

Vocabulary extension

1 Find some words in the text that can have different meanings, e.g. 'cross', 'sheet' and 'fold'. Compose some sentences demonstrating the different meanings of the words.

Related texts:

'50 Gardening Projects for Kids' by Clare Bradley

'Little Green Fingers' by Mary An Van Hage

'101 Things to Make' by Juliet Bawden

'Art Attack' by Neil Buchanan

The Great Flood

About the text

As well as creation stories, 'flood' stories are also common to a variety of cultures. This particular flood story is based on a native American legend.

Key Stage 2
Literacy Poster Pack 3

Letts
EDUCATIONAL

The Great Flood

Long, long ago, the Great Spirit lived on the snowy summit of Takhoma. He became very angry with the people and animals of his world because they were wicked and did many bad things to each other. He decided that he would rid the earth of them all except the good animals and one good man and his family.

So he said to the good man, "Shoot an arrow into that cloud hanging low over the mountain." The good man shot an arrow and it stuck in the cloud. "Now shoot another arrow into the shaft of that arrow," continued the Great Spirit. The second arrow hit the lower part of the first arrow and stuck there. The man kept on shooting arrows and after a while there was a long rope of arrows reaching from the cloud on top of the mountain down to the ground.

"Now tell your wife and children," commanded the Great Spirit, "to climb up that rope of arrows. Tell the good animals to climb up after them. But don't let the bad people and bad animals climb up."

So the good man sent his wife up the arrow rope, then his children, then the good animals. Then the good man himself climbed up. Just as he was stepping into the cloud he looked back. Coming up the arrow rope was a long line of bad animals and snakes. So the good man broke the rope and watched them all tumble down the side of the mountain.

Then the Great Spirit caused a heavy rain to fall. It rained and rained and rained for many days and nights. All the earth was under water. The water rose higher and higher on the sides of Takhoma. At last it came up to the snow line, up to the high place where the snow leaves off in the summer time. By that time all the bad people and bad animals were drowned so the Great Spirit commanded the rain to stop. He and the good man watched the waters go slowly down. The land became dry again.

Then the Great Spirit said to the good man, "Now you may take your family and animals back to the earth." So they all climbed out of the cloud, and the good man led them down a mountain trail to the place where they were to build a new lodge. As they walked down they found no bad animals or snakes, and there have been none on Takhoma to this day.

From Indian Legends of the Pacific Northwest by Ella Clark

© Letts Educational 1998   See *Letts Literacy Activity Book 3*   page 56

Teaching opportunities at:

TEXT Level
Reading comprehension

1 Many children will be familiar with the story of Noah. Ask the children to recall and recount it in their own words as a lead-in to this story. Having read the story on the poster, compare similarities of theme and content. Ask the children to suggest what the theme of the story is. *(Good over evil.)*

2 How 'true' do the children think the actual story is? Does it matter? What would be important to the people to whom it was told (passed on orally). *(Answers will depend on the children's interpretation.)*

3 Discuss what can be learned about the 'Great Spirit' from the passage. Do we learn what he looks like? How he sounds? Is he 'good' or 'bad'? *(Answers will depend on the children's interpretation.)*

4 Whilst reading the story, ask the children to identify any traditional story language, for example, 'Long, long ago', 'to this day'.

Writing composition

1 The story is clearly structured in paragraphs and events. Ask the children to suggest the main point of each part of the story and list these on the board, to develop a story plan or framework in note form in fairly general terms. *(The Great Spirit is cross → he asks a good man to shoot an arrow into a cloud, then another arrow into that, and so on → the Great Spirit tells the man and his wife and the good animals to climb the arrow rope → they climb up → the Great Spirit causes a flood → the flood stops → the good man, his family and the good animals climb down.)*

2 Encourage the children to use this framework as a basis for developing their own 'flood' story, using the same story theme but substituting different characters and settings.

SENTENCE Level
Grammatical awareness

1 Identify and list all the adjectives in the story. Note how they enhance the quality of the writing by giving more information about nouns. *(There are many to choose from.)* Make a list of alternative adjectives which could be used instead. Remind the children that words with similar meanings are called synonyms.

Sentence construction and punctuation

1 Experiment with sentences in the extract, by changing the word order within them. Ask the children to consider which combinations and sequences are possible, which affect the meaning, and which do not, for example, 'The Great Spirit lived on the mountain.' 'On the mountain lived the Great Spirit.' 'Lived the Great Spirit on the mountain?'

WORD Level
Spelling

1 Investigate how adjectives change when they are compared, e.g. 'high', 'higher', 'highest'; 'snowy', 'snowier', 'snowiest'; 'sad', 'sadder', 'saddest', etc. Link the work to the adjectives in the extract and use them for comparative purposes.

2 Ask the children to look for words in the passage that have been suffixed in some way, such as 'commanded'. Investigate what the root word is in each case and whether its spelling has been changed in any way. *(In this case, 'command + ed', with no spelling change.)*

Vocabulary extension

1 Ask the children to find sets of five words from the text beginning with the same letter. Practise ordering these words alphabetically according to the second letter and, perhaps, the third.

2 Hold dictionary challenges, encouraging children to find specific words from the text in the shortest possible time in their dictionaries.

Related texts:

'The American Indians' by Alain Quesnal

'How the World Began and Other Stories of Creation' by Andrew Matthews

'An Illustrated Treasury of Myths and Legends' by James Riordan

'Native North American Stories' by Robert Hull

'How Rabbit Stole The Fire: A Folk Tale From North America' by Joanna Troughton

On the Run

About the text

This short passage is taken from an exciting adventure story of the same name, written by Nina Bawden.

Teaching opportunities at:

TEXT Level
Reading comprehension

1 Read the introduction and look at the illustration. Ask the children what they think is going to happen. *(Answers will depend on the children's interpretation.)*

2 Read the story with expression, bringing out its suspense-filled nature. Spend some time investigating how the writer builds up the suspense by studying the opening, the build-up of atmosphere and the way language is used to create tension, especially the use of adjectives, similes, powerful verbs, etc.

3 Draw attention to the way Ben's feelings are portrayed. Ask the children to suggest words describing his feelings and to suggest the sorts of things he might have been thinking. Ask the children to relate any similar experiences they have had of noises in the night, creeping and not wanting to be heard, etc. *(Treat this issue sensitively as some children may find this difficult.)*

4 What sort of picture have the children built up of the house? Ask them to describe it and then to check the description against facts explicitly stated in the text. *(The facts are that the house has square windows, an iron fire escape, the ground and first floor and at least one bedroom.)*

Writing composition

1 The story is left as a cliff-hanger. Ask the children to continue it in their own words, building on from the known situation. Encourage them to try and maintain the tension by good use of descriptive language and some intimation of the emotions experienced.

2 Allow the children to retell the passage again as if they were Ben, by making it a first-person narrative.

Key Stage 2
Literacy Poster Pack 3

Letts EDUCATIONAL

On the Run

Thomas comes from a country in Africa. His father, who was Prime Minister there, is in prison in England. Thomas is staying in England and has made friends with a boy called Ben. The two boys suspect that Thomas is in danger from his uncles and Miss Fisher who look after him. Ben decides to help Thomas escape.

Ben moved cautiously towards the house. All the windows were dark; black squares in the blackness of the house wall. Ben stood at the foot of the fire-escape, looking up. Perhaps he could find Thomas' bedroom. Thomas was almost certain to be in bed by now. Miss Fisher wasn't the sort of woman to let a boy stay up late. If he could find Thomas' bedroom he could tell him the good news and go straight home, quick and silent as a thief in the night...

But as he climbed the first flight of rusty iron stairs, Ben's heart was pounding. Suppose Miss Fisher were to catch him – or one of the uncles. The terrible Uncle Tuku in his chief's robes! Ben thought about Uncle Tuku and moved more slowly; with each step he took his feet seemed to grow heavier until it was like heaving two balls of lead. Once he kicked a little stone that had somehow got onto the fire-escape and it rattled down and down, with a dreadful, ear-splitting, heart-stopping sound. Ben stood still, half expecting all the windows in the house to blaze suddenly with light. None of them did.

On the first floor, the lower half of a window was open. He peered in. It was dark inside and the drawn curtains were heavy and thick, moving only very little in the light breeze. For a moment he waited, shivering, although the night was warm. Then he thought of Thomas, lying awake in the dark and worrying about his father, and pulled himself up, over the window-sill.

As his feet touched the floor inside the room, the light was switched on.

He stood, so rigid with fright that for a moment or two, though he heard voices, he had no idea what they were saying. He just closed his eyes and waited – waited for the curtains to be torn open, for the certain discovery. But...

Nina Bawden

© Letts Educational 1998   See *Letts Literacy Activity Book 3*   page 62

SENTENCE Level
Grammatical awareness

1 Read the passage again and point out all the pronouns in it. *('He', 'him', 'it', 'his' and 'them'.)* On each occasion, ask the children who, or what, each pronoun stands for. Explain that a pronoun is a word that stands in place of a noun ('pro' means 'in place of'). Reread each sentence and replace each pronoun with the noun that it stands for, to demonstrate how the use of pronouns avoids too much repetition. *(e.g. Then Ben thought of Thomas, lying awake in the dark and worrying about Thomas' father...)*

Sentence construction and punctuation

1 Hold a punctuation mark hunt. Ask the children to read the extract and find all the full stops, commas and exclamation marks. Ask them to explain what function they serve.

WORD Level
Spelling

1 Select a range of words from the passage and give them to the children. Ask them to see how many smaller words they can find in each word, e.g. discovery = disc, is, cover, over, very.

2 Hold a spelling pattern word hunt. Provide the children with a number of specific letter patterns, e.g. 'un', 'ow', 'igh', etc. Ask the children to find as many words as possible in the passage containing those letter patterns. *('Un': 'country', 'uncle', 'pounding', 'sound'; 'ow': 'now', 'slowly', 'somehow', 'down', 'window'; 'igh': 'straight', 'night', 'light', 'flight', 'fright'.)*

Vocabulary extension

1 Ask the children to select a number of words they found interesting in the passage and to compose their own sentences using these words, to show that they understand their meanings and how to use them properly. Check the meanings in a dictionary.

Related texts:

Other suggested titles by Nina Bawden:

'Carrie's War' (for fluent readers)

'The Runaway Summer'

'The White Horse Gang'

'Witch's Daughter'

NB Nina Bawden's books are ideal for proficient readers. However, her books are always appropriate for reading to a class, especially for stimulating discussion.

Fantastic Mr Fox

About the text

This extract comes from one of Roald Dahl's best-selling stories, about a wily fox and three farmers who are determined to get him.

Key Stage 2
Literacy Poster Pack 3

Fantastic Mr Fox

The three farmers are angry with Mr Fox because he steals from them to feed his family. They decide to hide outside his fox hole and shoot him when he comes out.

"Don't get careless," said Mrs Fox. "You know they'll be waiting for you, all three of them."

"Don't worry about me," said Mr Fox. "I'll see you later."

But Mr Fox would not have been quite so cocky had he known exactly where the three farmers were waiting at that moment. They were just outside the entrance to the hole, each one crouching behind a tree with his gun loaded. And what is more, they had chosen their positions very carefully, making sure that the wind was not blowing from them towards the fox's hole. In fact, it was blowing in the opposite direction. There was no chance of them being 'smelled out'.

Mr Fox crept up the dark tunnel to the mouth of his hole. He poked his long handsome face out into the night air and sniffed once.

He moved an inch or two forward and stopped. He sniffed again. He was always especially careful when coming out of his hole.

He inched forward a little more. The front half of his body was now in the open.

His black nose twitched from side to side, sniffing and sniffing for the scent of danger. He found none, and he was just about to go trotting forward into the wood when he heard, or thought he heard a tiny noise, a soft rustling sound, as though someone had moved a foot ever so gently through a patch of dry leaves.

Mr Fox flattened his body against the ground and lay very still, his ears pricked. He waited a long time, but he heard nothing more.

"It must have been a field-mouse," he told himself, "or some other small animal."

He crept a little further out of the hole... then further still. He was almost right out in the open now. He took a last careful look around. The wood was murky and very still. Somewhere in the sky the moon was shining.

Just then, his sharp night-eyes caught a glint of something bright behind a tree not far away. It was a small silver speck of moonlight shining on a polished surface. Mr Fox lay still, watching it. What on earth was it? Now it was moving. It was coming up and up... Great heavens! It was the barrel of a gun! Quick as a whip, Mr Fox jumped back in his hole and at the same time the entire wood seemed to explode around him.

Roald Dahl

© Letts Educational 1998

See *Letts Literacy Activity Book 3* page 64

Teaching opportunities at:

TEXT Level
Reading comprehension

1 Draw attention to the fact that the passage is from a book by Roald Dahl. Ask the children to talk about any other books of his they have read and to comment on them and Roald Dahl as an author.

2 Read the title and the introduction. Ask the children what they think the passage is going to be about and what they infer from the title. Will the fox get caught or will he get the upper hand? *(Answers will depend on the children's interpretation.)*

3 After reading the extract, list what can be learned about the farmers and about Mr Fox. What do we know about them as characters? In what way do both display considerable guile and cunning? What words could be used to describe them? How do they behave? *(Answers will depend on the children's interpretation.)*

4 Consider the credibility of the events – might the farmers have a case against the fox? *(It is likely.)* Do foxes steal chickens from farms? *(They do steal.)* Why? *(For food.)*

5 Consider and discuss together the skillful way in which Roald Dahl builds up an atmosphere of tension by using powerful language, and the way he describes events.

Writing composition

1 Children could be asked to plan and write an episode from 'Fantastic Mr Fox's' continual battle of wits with the farmers. Encourage them to set their work out in paragraphs and to include descriptive words and dialogue. These could be made into an anthology, each story with its own heading, author details, etc.

2 Ask the children to write a review of the passage, giving details of what the story is about, their opinions of the characters and what they liked or disliked about the author's style and way of writing.

SENTENCE Level
Grammatical awareness

1 Reread the passage and point out all the pronouns in it. *('They', 'you', 'them', 'me', 'I', 'he', 'his', 'their', 'it' and 'him'.)* On each occasion, ask the children who, or what, each pronoun stands for. Explain that a pronoun is a word that stands in place of a noun ('pro' means 'in place of'). Reread each sentence and replace each pronoun with the noun that it stands for, to demonstrate how the use of pronouns avoids too much repetition.

2 Discuss which of the pronouns are personal pronouns. *('I', 'you', 'he', 'she', 'they', 'them' and 'me'.)* And which are possessive. *('My', 'his' and 'their'.)* Construct some sentences using both forms in them.

3 Draw attention to how pronouns are used to mark gender for example, 'Mr Fox' is 'he', Mrs Fox is 'she', etc. What gender are the farmers? Do we know if they are all the same gender? *(We can infer they are all male from the pronoun 'his' with gun.)*

Sentence construction and punctuation

1 Point out the use of common conjunctions to join single sentences together, to make longer, complex sentences. *('But', 'and' and 'then'.)* Split the sentences up into shorter ones by removing the conjunctions.

2 Provide pairs of sentences and ask the children to find ways of combining them into one longer sentence. Explore what changes occur.

WORD Level
Spelling

1 Find the word 'explode' in the extract. Ask the children to suggest other words with the 'ex-' prefix. Use a dictionary to help. *(There are many possible answers.)* Note how root words may have the prefix added to them and how this may affect their meaning.

2 Carry out similar exercises with other words with prefixes, such as 'mis-', 'non-', 'co-' and 'anti-'. Suggest the children practise their spellings using the 'Look, say, cover, write, check' method.

Vocabulary extension

1 Ask the children what the difference is between the homonyms 'fowl' and 'foul'. *(They sound the same but are spelled differently and mean different things.)* Investigate other words that sound the same but are spelled differently, e.g. 'wood' and 'would', etc.

2 Investigate words which are spelled the same but have two meanings, e.g. 'soaps', 'wave', 'bank', etc. Make a class table, perhaps with illustrations for clarity.

Related texts:

Other Roald Dahl suggestions:

'Boy: Tales of Childhood'

'Charlie and the Chocolate Factory'

'James and the Giant Peach'

'The Magic Finger'

'The Witches'

'Matilda'

Other fox/wolf stories that might be appropriate:

'Foxy Fables' by Tony Ross

'The True Story of the Three Little Pigs by A Wolf' by Jon Scieszka and Lane Smith

'The Fox Busters' by Dick King Smith

'Last Stories of Polly and the Wolf' by Catherine Storr

NB Children may be interested in the book 'Roald Dahl' by John Malam.

Sophie Meets the BFG

About the poster

This extract is taken from one of the most popular children's books by best-selling author, Roald Dahl. As well as the extract, there is also some biographical information about Roald Dahl himself.

Teaching opportunities at:

TEXT Level
Reading comprehension

1 Who is the BFG? *(The Big Friendly Giant.)* What can be learned about him from the passage? Is he as fearsome as he seems at first? *(Answers will depend on the children's interpretation.)* What is unusual about the way he talks? *(The way he invents his own words.)*

2 How does Sophie respond to the BFG? *(She is scared but grows angry.)* What evidence is there telling us how she feels? *(By her response to what the giant says.)*

3 What words does the author use to build up a rather frightening atmosphere? *(For example, 'the trembling Sophie', 'the Giant boomed', etc.)*

4 Ask the children what other Roald Dahl books they have read. Keep a running list of books written by him. Ask the children to add additional titles as they come up with them.

5 Discuss what information children found interesting in the biography about Roald Dahl.

6 Talk about the differences in style and language used in the factual passage and the story. *(The factual passage is objective, impersonal, full of facts, has no dialogue and is biographical. The story is full of action, dialogue and is about imaginary characters.)*

Key Stage 2
Literacy Poster Pack 3

Letts EDUCATIONAL

Sophie Meets the BFG

The Giant picked up the trembling Sophie with one hand and carried her across the cave and put her on the table. Now he really is going to eat me, Sophie thought.

The Giant sat down and stared hard at Sophie. He had truly enormous ears. Each one was as big as the wheel of a truck and he seemed to be able to move them onwards and outwards from his head as he wished.

"I is hungry!" the Giant boomed. He grinned, showing massive square teeth. The teeth were very white and square and they sat in his mouth like huge slices of white bread.

"P...Please don't eat me," Sophie stammered.

The Giant let out a bellow of laughter.

"Just because I is a Giant, you think I is a man-gobbling cannybull!" he shouted. "You is about right! Giants is all cannybully and murderful! And they does eat up human beans! We is in Giant Country now! Giants is everywhere around! Out there us has

the famous Bonecrunching Giant! Bonecrunching Giant crunches up two wopsey whiffling human beans for supper every night! Noise is earbursting! Noise of crunching bones goes crackety-crack for miles around!"

"Ouch!" said Sophie.

"Bonecrunching Giant only gobbles human beans from Turkey," the Giant said. "Every night Bonecruncher is galloping off to Turkey to gobble Turks."

Sophie's sense of patriotism was so bruised by this remark that she became quite angry. "Why Turks?" she blurted out. "What's wrong with the English?"

"Bonecrunching Giant says Turks is tasting oh ever so much juicier and more scrumdiddlyumptious! Bonecruncher says Turkish human beans has a glamoury flavour. He says Turks from Turkey is tasting of turkey."

From The BFG by Roald Dahl

Roald Dahl is one of the most popular children's authors in the world. Roald didn't much enjoy school himself, and found teachers too strict. Before taking up writing, Roald led an adventurous life, spending time in Africa, tangling with animals and crashing a plane during the war. When Roald found he had a talent for writing he never looked back. Roald had a sense of humour that appeals to children and loved being rude. *Charlie and the Chocolate Factory* is one of the best-selling books of all time. Other favourites include *The BFG, Revolting Rhymes* and *Fantastic Mr Fox.*

© Letts Educational 1998   See *Letts Literacy Activity Book 3* page 66

Writing composition

1 Ask the children to write a description of the BFG based on information in the text and their imagination.

2 Ask the children to write a personal review of the passage, explaining briefly what it is about, and what they liked or disliked about it.

3 Have fun making up words the BFG might say. Make up sentences about how people from other countries might taste, e.g. Poland, Greece, Russia, etc. (Tread carefully here to avoid any racism or clumsy stereotyping. Be sensitive to how some children might feel.)

4 Use the biographical details of Roald Dahl as an opportunity for writing some notes on key facts. Point out that the biography is core information with little padding.

SENTENCE Level
Grammatical awareness

1 Use the text as a way to introduce adjectives describing nationalities, e.g. a Turkish person comes from Turkey. You might mark up a wall map with these.

2 Identify the use of pronouns in the passage, and explain what the word pronoun means ('pro' means 'in place of', so a 'pronoun' is used in place of a 'noun'.) Demonstrate how pronouns are used to prevent a lot of unnecessary repetition in the text, by reading the first sentence and substituting Sophie's name for the relevant pronouns, e.g. 'The Giant picked up the trembling Sophie with one hand and carried Sophie (her) across the cave and put Sophie (her) on the table'.

3 Give the children a list of common personal pronouns, e.g. 'I', 'we', 'you', 'he', 'she', 'it', 'they', 'him', 'her', 'them', etc. Ask them to find examples in the text and to say who or what each pronoun stands for. *(Answers will depend on the section chosen.)*

4 The passage is ideal for investigating grammatical agreement between pronouns and verbs. Discuss the way the Giant speaks and correct the grammatical agreement of his sentences.

Sentence construction and punctuation

1 Draw attention to the speech marks in the passage and the way in which exclamation marks are used for emphasis.

2 Use some of the sentences in the text to focus on conjunctions joining two shorter sentences, making them into one longer sentence. Provide the children with the beginnings of sentences which include the conjunction, and ask them to provide some sensible endings. e.g. 'Sophie wondered if...'. Use conjunctions like 'so', 'and', 'while', 'though', 'since' and 'when'.

WORD Level
Spelling

1 The Giant uses a lot of nonsense words and words that are misspelled. Ask the children to look in a dictionary and find other words that begin with the prefixes 'mis-' and 'non-'.

2 Copy some of the Giant's invented words and look for smaller words within them. *(Answers will depend on the section chosen.)* This will help the children to learn spellings.

3 Brainstorm and list words which end with the suffix '-ful'. Work out what the root noun of each is. The Giant often makes up 'ful' words, like 'murderful', by adding the suffix to words where it doesn't normally go. Have fun making up some more Giant words ending in '-ful'.

4 Give the children some common phonemes or letter strings, e.g. 'ea' or 'oo', and set them word hunts to find words in the passage containing them. *(For example, 'eat' and 'boomed'.)*

Vocabulary extension

1 Gather 'dialogue' words from the text, e.g. 'stammered', 'bellowed', 'boomed'. Ask the children to add as many more dialogue words to the list as they can by looking in other texts.

2 Select some interesting (but real) words from the passage and ask the children to look up their meanings in a class dictionary, e.g. 'patriotism', 'bruised', 'talent', etc.

3 Select and list some words and ask the children to find synonyms for them in a thesaurus.

Related texts:

Other Roald Dahl suggestions:
'Charlie and the Chocolate Factory'
'James and the Giant Peach'
'The Magic Finger'
'The Witches'
'Matilda'
NB Children may be interested in the book 'Roald Dahl' by John Malam.

Treasure Island

About the text

This extract is taken from the classic tale of adventure, intrigue and piracy by Robert Louis Stevenson.

Key Stage 2
Literacy Poster Pack 3

Letts
EDUCATIONAL

Treasure Island

This is the famous story told by young Jim Hawkins of how he finds a treasure map belonging to the notorious pirate, Captain Flint. Jim sets sail on the good ship Hispaniola with Squire Trelawney and Captain Smollett to find the treasure. The ship's cook, Long John Silver, plans to double-cross them.

Treasure Island looked a gloomy, forbidding place. The lower parts were wooded, with rocky peaks jutting above the trees. Even in the sunshine, with birds soaring above, I hated the thought of it. We were anchored in an inlet where trees came down to the water. The air was hot and still, and the men were restless and grumbling. Captain Smollett gave leave for the men to go ashore, which raised their spirits. I believe the silly fellows thought they would break their shins over treasure as soon as they landed. Long John Silver was in charge of the two boats taking the thirteen men ashore. I knew I should not be needed on board so I decided to go ashore too.

I ran up the beach into the woods, glad to be free and alone. I sat quietly hidden in the bushes. Hearing voices, I moved nearer to catch the words. I could see and hear Long John Silver bullying a sailor to join him and the pirates. The sailor angrily refused. Silver's answer was to plunge his dagger into the man and leave him lying dead in the forest. I felt faint and the whole world swam around me in a whirling mist. When I pulled myself together, Silver, crutch under his arm, was wiping his knife on a tuft of grass. I feared for my life if I should be found, and ran and ran, not caring where.

When I stopped I was at the foot of a stony hill. My eye was caught by a movement on the hillside. I could not tell if it was a man or an animal. Here was a new danger I felt I could not face, and I began to run towards the shore. But the creature was faster than me and, darting from tree to tree, he came closer. I could now see that it was a man, but so wild and strange that I was afraid. As he neared me he threw himself on the ground, and held up his hands as if begging for mercy. I have never seen such a ragged creature. He was dressed in patchwork of odd clothes and goat skins, and his blue eyes looked startling in a face burned black by the sun.

Adapted from the story by Robert Louis Stevenson

© Letts Educational 1998   See *Letts Literacy Activity Book 3* page 68

Teaching opportunities at:

TEXT Level
Reading comprehension

1 Many children may have read the book before or seen the film or video. Ask the class to talk about any prior knowledge they have to help set the extract in context as an exciting adventure.

2 Read the introduction and title and look at the illustration. What clues are there that the story took place some time ago? *(The story is a classic tale, so must have taken place a while ago. The ship is pictured as a wooden sailboat, the picture of pirates (as portrayed here) is old fashioned, etc.)*

3 Discuss what can be discovered about Jim's character and feelings and those of Long John Silver from information explicitly stated in the text, or by deduction. *(Answers will depend on the children's interpretation but specifically we learn he hates the thought of the island, he feels faint, he is scared, etc.)*

Writing composition

1 The theme of pirates, treachery and treasure is an excellent stimulus for story writing. Children could write their own versions of how the story might continue or make up their own characters and settings. Encourage them to use lots of dramatic language and to try to keep the suspense alive.

2 Refer back to the opening paragraph of the passage and note how the scene is set by the use of good descriptive language to create an effect of tension. Encourage children to write an exciting opening to an adventure story using the same techniques.

SENTENCE Level
Grammatical awareness

1 Notice that the story is told by young Jim Hawkins in the form of a personal account or diary. It is told in the first-person 'I' – unlike most stories which are told in the third-person. Take a paragraph from the story and rewrite it in the third-person, noting what changes occur. *(Answers will depend on the section chosen.)*

Sentence construction and punctuation

1 Point out the use of common conjunctions to join single sentences together, to make longer, complex sentences in the passage, for example, 'so', 'and', 'but', etc. Try rewriting these as single, simple sentences and notice the difference this makes. Alternatively, give the children a series of short sentences and ask them to use conjunctions to make them longer.

Related texts:

'Kidnapped' by R L Stevenson

'Sinbad the Sailor and Other Tales from the Arabian Nights' retold by N J Dawood

Less difficult stories:

'The Great Piratical Rumbustification and the Library and the Robbers' by Margaret Mahy

'King Keith and the Jolly Lodger' by Kaye Umansky (a lovely fun story about Roger the pirate)

The 'Captain Pugwash' series by John Ryan (very suitable for reluctant readers)

WORD Level
Spelling

1 Use the words in the passage, or part of the passage, as a means of reviewing work on syllables. Decide which are one, two and three-syllable words. Write the multi-syllabic words and establish where the syllable boundaries are within them. *(Answers will depend on the section chosen.)*

2 Hold a treasure hunt for common letter patterns, such as 'ure', 'ie', 'ir', etc. Put a list of letter patterns on the board and ask the children to find as many words as possible from the text containing them. *(For example, 'treas<u>ure</u>', 'qu<u>ie</u>tly', 'p<u>ir</u>ates', etc.)*

Vocabulary extension

1 Select some of the more interesting or tricky words (use adjectives, nouns and verbs) from the passage. Ask the children to define them by using a dictionary and then to look for their synonyms in a thesaurus.

2 Find the word 'board' in the extract. Ask the children the difference between this and the word 'bored'. *(They sound the same, but are spelled differently and mean different things.)* Ask the children to suggest other homonyms for the following words from the passage and to explain their meanings: 'peak', 'place', 'told', 'sail', 'find', 'break', 'need', 'beach', 'faint', 'whole', 'mist', 'shore' and 'blue'. *('Peek', 'plaice', 'tolled', 'sale', 'fined', 'brake', 'kneed', 'beech', 'feint', 'hole', 'missed', 'sure' and 'blew'.)*

Face to Face with a Tiger

About the text

This is a first-hand account of a real-life adventure in Nepal.

Key Stage 2
Literacy Poster Pack 3

Letts EDUCATIONAL

Face to Face with a Tiger

This article comes from a magazine called It happened to me! *in which readers write in with extraordinary things that have happened to them. In it, Tony Russell describes how he will never forget the tiger he met in Nepal.*

Last year I went to Nepal for three months to work in a hospital. I think it's important to see as much of the country as you can, but it is difficult to travel around Nepal. The hospital let me have a few days' holiday, so I decided to go into the jungle and I asked a Nepalese guide, Kamal Rai, to go with me.

We started preparing for the trip at six in the morning, and left camp with two elephants carrying our equipment. It was hot, but Kamal made me wear shoes and trousers to protect me from snakes. In the jungle there was a lot of wildlife, but we were trying to find big cats, especially tigers.

We climbed onto the elephants' backs to get a better view, but it is unusual to find tigers in the afternoon because they sleep in the heat of the day.

Then, in the distance, we saw a tiger, and Kamal told me to be very quiet. We crept a little nearer and found a dead deer, still bleeding! This was the tiger's lunch! Suddenly I started to feel very frightened.

We heard the tiger a second before we saw it. It jumped out like a flash of lightning, over five hundred kilos in weight and four metres long. I looked into its eyes and face, and saw right down the animal's throat. It grabbed Kamal's leg between its teeth, but I managed to pull Kamal away. One of our elephants ran at the tiger and made it go back into the grass, so we quickly escaped to let the tiger eat its lunch. That night it was impossible to sleep!

© Letts Educational 1998   See *Letts Literacy Activity Book 3* page 70

Teaching opportunities at:

TEXT Level
Reading comprehension

1 Read the extract. Discuss the way it is set out. *(It is in columns.)* How can you tell this came from a magazine rather than a story book? How is the presentation different? *(Books are not usually written in columns like this.)*

2 Who wrote the article? *(Tony Russell.)* Discuss what factual information it contains. *(There are many possible answers.)*

3 Ask the children to recount the adventure in sequence in their own words.

4 Discuss what Tony's thoughts and feelings might have been at different points throughout the story. *(Answers will depend on the children's interpretation.)*

5 Ask the children to evaluate his behaviour – was he sensible? Foolish? Brave? *(Answers will depend on the children's interpretation.)*

6 Ask the children whether they think this really happened or not, and to justify their opinions.

7 Find other true-life adventures in newspapers and magazines. Read, compare and contrast them.

Writing composition

1 Use the article as a model. Ask the children to make up their own true-life adventure. Brainstorm ideas, such as 'The day I met the Abominable Snowman', etc. Lay them out in paragraphs and columns like in a newspaper or magazine. They could be word-processed which would give them more 'authenticity' by using different type sizes and styles. Collate them into a collection or magazine-style presentation, perhaps with pictures or illustrations. Write them as first-person accounts.

SENTENCE Level
Grammatical awareness

1 Try converting the article into the third-person and discuss any changes that are needed – to pronouns, verb agreements, etc. *(For example, 'Last year Tony Russell went to Nepal', etc.)*

2 Identify the pronouns in the article and decide if they are personal or possessive pronouns, and are singular or plural. *(Personal: 'I', 'it', 'me', 'we', 'they'; possessive: 'its' and 'our'.)* Write some sentences which contain both types of pronoun.

Sentence construction and punctuation

1 Point out the use of common conjunctions in the passage to join single sentences together, to make longer, complex sentences, such as 'so', 'and', 'but', 'then', etc. Try rewriting these as single, simple sentences and notice the difference this makes. Or, alternatively, provide the children with some short sentences and ask them to make longer ones.

WORD Level
Spelling

1 Investigate how adjectives change when they are used for comparison, e.g. 'near', 'nearer', 'nearest'; 'heavy', 'heavier', 'heaviest'; 'hot', 'hotter', 'hottest', etc., linking the work to the adjectives in the text.

2 Ask the children to look for words in the passage that have been suffixed in some way, for example, 'carrying' or 'carry + ing'. Investigate what the root word is in each case and whether its spelling has been changed in any way. *(There are many possible examples.)*

Vocabulary extension

1 What warning might Tony have shouted to Kamal when he saw the tiger? *(Answers will depend on the children's interpretation.)* Think of other situations in which warnings might need to be given. What common expressions are often used in these circumstances? *(There are many possible answers.)* Use this as an opportunity to discuss expressions commonly used to express surprise, apology, greeting, thanks, refusal, etc.

Related texts:

The following fiction titles may be of use for extra flavour of the region:

'The Wizard Punchkin: A Folk Tale from India' by Joanna Troughton

'The Prince and the Flying Carpet' retold by Margaret Mayo (from the 'Orchard Book of Magical Tales')

'Just So Stories' by Rudyard Kipling

Poems for Fun

About the poster

The four poems and rhymes on the poster are full of humour and fun. 'The Adventures of Isabel' by Ogden Nash is about a girl who was not perturbed by anything, even when she met a hungry bear. 'The Flea and the Fly' is full of alliteration and is quite a tongue-twister. 'The Tale of the Poor Peanut' is pure nonsense. And 'It's a Puzzle!' is full of puns and word play.

Key Stage 2
Literacy Poster Pack 3
Letts EDUCATIONAL

Poems for Fun

The Adventures of Isabel
Isabel met an enormous bear,
Isabel, Isabel, didn't care;
The bear was hungry, the bear was ravenous,
The bear's big mouth was cruel and cavernous.
The bear said, "Isabel, pleased to meet you.
How do, Isabel, now I'll eat you!"
Isabel, Isabel, didn't worry,
Isabel didn't scream or scurry,
She washed her hands and she straightened her hair up,
Then Isabel quietly ate the bear up!
Ogden Nash

The Flea and the Fly
A fly and a flea in a flue
Were wondering what they should do.
Said the fly, "Let us flee!"
Said the flea, "Let us fly!"
So they flew through a flaw in the flue!

The Tale of the Poor Peanut
A peanut sat on the railway track
Its heart was all a-flutter.
Along came a train, the 10.15 –
Toot! Toot! – peanut butter!

It's a Puzzle!
Where can a man buy a cap for his knee
Or a key for the lock of his hair?
And can the eyes be called a school?
I should think so – there are some pupils there!

© Letts Educational 1998   See *Letts Literacy Activity Book 3* page 76

Teaching opportunities at:

Text Level
Reading comprehension

1 Have fun reading the poems together. 'The Adventures of Isabel' lends itself well as a performance poem and could involve a degree of acting – one person or group taking the storyteller's part and another taking the bear's part. Attention to punctuation and expression are vital to get the most out of this poem. Similarly, parts of 'The Flea and the Fly' could also be read by different people. Encourage the children to try and read it as fast as possible. 'The Tale of the Poor Peanut' involves sound effects. 'It's à Puzzle!' makes interesting reading because it comprises two questions and an exclamation.

2 Ask the children what sort of girl they think Isabel is? *(Answers will depend on the children's interpretation.)* In what way is her response to the bear unexpected? *(Isabel isn't at all frightened.)* Why is this poem effective? *(It is unexpected role reversal with a strong female character.)* Discuss the poet's use of words to create effect, e.g. 'ravenous', 'cruel' and 'cavernous'. You might try to find other Ogden Nash poems to read.

3 Discuss the way words and sounds are used for effect in 'The Flea and the Fly'. Ask why rhymes like these are called 'tongue-twisters'. *(Because they are very hard to read quickly.)* Find and read other tongue-twisters.

4 Ask the children to use inference and deduction to explain what 'The Tale of the Poor Peanut' actually means. *(Answers will depend on the children's interpretation.)*

5 What is the appeal of 'It's a Puzzle!'? Is it a poem or a rhyme? In what sense could it be called 'word play'? *(It uses common words in unusual contexts.)*

6 Ask the children to express their opinions on the selection of poems. Which did they prefer? Why? In what way are they all different?

7 Encourage the children to look for other examples of humorous rhymes and poetry.

Writing composition

1 Think of other frightening situations Isabel might find herself in. Make up a poem about her likely reactions.

2 Encourage the children to make up other nonsense rhymes and word puzzles of their own or to make up tongue twisters.

SENTENCE Level
Grammatical awareness

1 'The Adventures of Isabel' is excellent for work on adjectives. Draw attention to how the adjectives are used to describe the bear. ('Enormous', 'hungry', 'big', 'ravenous', 'cruel' and 'cavernous'.) Focus attention on them by asking children to describe the bear. Copy out the first section of the poem and delete the adjectives. Discuss the difference this makes.

2 'The Adventures of Isabel' also provides lots of opportunities for work on verbs in a similar way to that above.

3 Use the poems to focus on pronouns. Find all of the pronouns in them and discuss who or what each pronoun represents. ('She' (Isabel), 'her (Isabel)', 'they (fly and flea)', 'its (peanut)' and 'I (author of poem)'.)

Sentence construction and punctuation

1 Ask the children to identify which poems or rhymes contain speech marks. Who is speaking in each case? ('The Adventures of Isabel' contains speech by the bear. 'The Flea and the Fly' contains speech by both the flea and the fly.) Which words are actually spoken? ('Isabel, pleased to meet you. How do, Isabel, now I'll eat you!'; 'Let us flee!', 'Let us fly.') Point out that only the words actually spoken go inside the speech marks. Point out the use of the comma, before the beginning of the actual dialogue, and the fact that the first word spoken each time begins with a capital letter.

WORD Level
Spelling

1 Examine the rhyming words and note how sometimes words which sound alike are not spelled alike. (For example, 'bear', 'care'; 'worry', 'scurry'; 'flue', 'do'; 'hair', 'there'.) Ask the children to think of some additional rhyming words.

2 Have fun making up sentences containing alliteration, e.g. 'The flying flag flipped and flapped'.

3 Find the examples of apostrophes being used in contractions in the extract. ('Didn't and I'll'.) What should the longer form of these contractions be? ('Did not' and 'I will'.) What letters are missed out? (The letters are 'o' and 'wi'.) Think of other contractions.

Vocabulary extension

1 What other words for parts of the body have two meanings? (For example, 'palm', 'crown' and 'calf'.)

2 Ask the children to write some sentences to show the difference in meaning between the following set of homonyms: 'through/threw'; 'bear/bare'; 'meet/meat'; 'ate/eight'; 'flee/flea'; 'flue/flew'; 'lock/loch'.

3 There are some good examples of synonyms in 'The Adventures of Isabel', for example, 'hungry' and 'ravenous'. Use a thesaurus to find synonyms for other words from the poster.

4 Note the way the bear greets Isabel. Discuss common expressions used for greeting people and bidding them goodbye.

Related texts:

'Custard and Company' by Ogden Nash
'Laughter is an Egg' by John Agard
'Rhymes and Riddles' by Fran Pickering
'Horace was a Happy Horse and Other Silly Verses' by Finola Akister
See also suggestions for Unit 1.2.

Writing Letters

About the poster

The Khan family are having a letter-writing session. Mr Khan is writing a letter to Shireen's teacher, Mrs Khan is word-processing a letter of complaint about a vacuum cleaner and Shireen is writing a thank-you letter to her Gran.

Key Stage 2
Literacy Poster Pack 3

Letts EDUCATIONAL

Writing Letters
Last week the Khan family each wrote a letter.

> 12 Ryman Avenue
> Bedford
> BD2 6TS
> December 4th
> 1998
>
> Dear Mrs James
> Shireen has to go to the dentist on Thursday at 2 o'clock. Would it be possible for me to pick her up after lunch?
>
> Yours sincerely
>
> *Reza Khan*
>
> Mr Reza Khan

> 12 Ryman Avenue
> Bedford
> BD2 6TS
> December 4th 1998
>
> Dear Sirs
> I recently bought one of your new Super Jet vacuum cleaners. I am not at all happy with it. One of the wheels was broken and it does not seem to suck up crumbs or dust very well. I am most disappointed. I really think you should do something about it urgently. I would welcome an early reply to my letter.
>
> Yours faithfully
>
> S. Khan
>
> Mrs S. Khan

> 12 Ryman Avenue
> Bedford
> BD2 6TS
> December 4th 1998
>
> Dear Gran
> Thank you for the money you sent me for my birthday. For months I have wanted a pair of pink trainers and now I will have enough money to get them. They will make me run even faster! I hope we can come and see you soon, then I can show you my trainers.
>
> Love
>
> Shireen

© Letts Educational 1998   *See Letts Literacy Activity Book 3* **page 78**

Teaching opportunities at:

TEXT Level
Reading comprehension

1 Read the letters and discuss the purpose of each. *(Answer will be found in 'About the poster' above.)*

2 Who is Mr Khan writing to? *(Mrs James.)* Why? *(To excuse Shireen from school to go to the dentist.)* What sort of a letter is it? *(A letter of request.)*

3 Who is Mrs Khan writing to? *(The vacuum cleaner manufacturer.)* What is Mrs Khan unhappy about? Why? *(One of the wheels has broken and it doesn't work very well.)* What sort of letter is it? *(A letter of complaint.)*

4 Why is Shireen writing to her Gran? *(To thank her for a birthday present.)* What sort of letter is she writing? *(A thank-you letter.)*

5 Discuss the main features of laying out a letter, which are common to all three letters. Where do the Khan's live? *(12 Ryman Avenue, Bedford.)* How is the address set out on each letter? *(It is in the top right-hand corner.)* Are there any differences in layout? Does it matter? *(The alignment is different.)* What date is it? *(4 December 1998.)* Where has the date been put? *(At the top of the letter.)* Why is it important? *(To allow for a response and so the recipient knows when the letter was sent.)* Who is each letter to? *(Mrs James; the*

vacuum manufacturer; Shireen's Gran.) Why has Mrs Khan not put the name of a person? *(She doesn't know the name.)*

6 How has each person 'signed off'? *('Yours sincerely', 'Yours faithfully', 'Love'.)* Discuss why they are all different. *(Levels of formality: 'Dear Sir' always partners 'Yours faithfully' and 'Dear Mr/s___' always partners 'Yours sincerely'.)*

7 Draw attention to the tone and degree of formality of each letter and discuss the reasons for the difference. Discuss how the style and vocabulary of each letter varies according to whom it is written. Which is the friendliest letter? *(Shireen's.)* Why? *(It is to a well-known member of her family.)* Which is the most formal letter? Why? *(Mrs Khan's because it is a complaint to someone she doesn't know.)*

8 Consider the reasons why Mrs Khan has chosen to type her letter, whereas the other two have handwritten theirs. *(For formality and clarity. The other two are more informal.)*

9 Think of other reasons why you might write to people. List them. *(There are many possible answers.)*

Writing composition

1 Encourage the children to compose and write letters of their own, using the structure and framework of those on the poster as a framework for their own writing. There are an endless number of imaginary situations that could be used as a vehicle for letter writing, but it is better, where possible, to make the situations as relevant and realistic as possible. Some suggestions are: a thank-you letter to someone in the school, e.g. a friend for helping, a teacher for being thoughtful, the caretaker for all he or she does to keep the school a pleasant place, etc.; a letter to parents about an event coming up, or explaining some work currently being undertaken; writing to an author about a book recently enjoyed; writing to someone inviting them to come into school to talk to the class.

2 Discuss some occasions when messages or notes need to be written, and the difference between these and letters. Think of practical situations within the class or school where notes or messages may be used.

SENTENCE Level
Grammatical awareness

1 Study the letters for the use of pronouns. Identify where they are used and who each stands for. *('Me', her', 'I', 'you', 'my' and 'we'.)* Discuss whether they are first-, second- or third-person pronouns, and whether they are singular or plural. *(Singular: 'me' (first), 'her' (second), 'I' (first), 'you' (second), 'my' (first); plural: 'you' (second), 'we' (first).)*

Sentence construction and punctuation

1 The conventions of punctuating the address and the finishing-off part of letters has changed with the advent of computers and personal preference. In the past, commas were more frequently used than they are now. Discuss this and consider whether it matters.

2 Spot where sentences have been joined by the conjunction 'and'. Try breaking these sentences down into shorter sentences.

WORD Level
Spelling

1 The texts of the letters could be used as a starting point to discuss how a good understanding of suffixes helps with spelling. Look for words with suffixes, like '-ly', '-er', '-ed', '-s', '-en' and '-ful'. Discuss what the root words are and how adding the suffix changes the spelling and/or meaning of each word.

2 Select some multisyllabic words from the poster and use them as a basis for breaking words into syllables, for example, 'den/tist'.

3 Ask the children to choose a few words they find difficult in the extract and to copy them and learn them using the 'Look, say, cover, write, check' method.

Vocabulary extension

1 Gather some letters and ask the children to note the different expressions that are used to 'sign off'. Categorise them as informal or formal and suggest when they might be used.

Related texts:

'Write Away: Keeping in Touch from Fan Mail to Faxes' by Viv Edwards

'Dear Mr Merlin' by Moira Andrew (a delightful poem from 'A Blue Poetry Paintbox', compiled by John Foster)

Information Books

About the text

This poster shows the front and back cover of an information book on sport, as well as the contents and index pages. It is useful for helping children understand the various features of information books and how to use them effectively.

Teaching opportunities at:

TEXT Level
Reading comprehension

1 Ensure that the children understand the difference between 'fiction' and 'non-fiction'. Discuss the purpose of information and reference books and the general reasons why children might refer to them.

2 How helpful is the cover of the book on the poster? What does it tell children? *(It gives the title and the author. The illustrations capture the contents of the book.)* What can be learned from the book 'blurb' on the back cover? *(This is a précis of what the book contains.)*

3 Look at the front and back covers of other reference books. Discuss, compare and evaluate recurring features.

4 Look at the contents page. What do such pages tell us in general? *(They explain the sections, or chapters, into which the book is divided.)* Ask some questions based on the contents page shown.

5 Follow the same pattern for the index page. Note how the entries are all in alphabetical order. Ask the children to practise scanning the page for specific information by asking questions about the page.

6 Sometimes contents and index pages do not mention what we are looking for, e.g. 'rounders'. Ask the children what this might

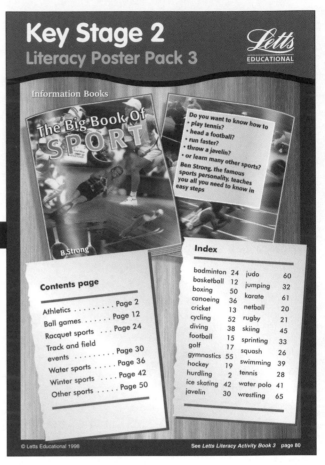

mean and what they might do next. *('Rounders' does not appear in the book. The children might then look in the index of another book.)*

7 Ask the children to suggest other books that are organised alphabetically, for instance, telephone directories, encyclopaedias and dictionaries.

Writing composition

1 Make a class information book on a topic of your choice, e.g. football, pop music, etc. Discuss what would go in such a book and how it would be organised. Work out the chapters and delegate the writing of different chapters to different groups. Consider issues of layout, paragraphing, illustration, pagination, etc. Collate the chapters into book form, write a contents page and work out what should go on the index page. Design a cover and book 'blurb'.

SENTENCE Level
Grammatical awareness

1 The topic of sport is useful for reviewing work on nouns and verbs. What equipment is needed for each sport? Where are such sports played? Who plays them? Ask the children to list appropriate nouns, for example, 'bats', 'balls', 'field', 'pool', etc. What do you do in each sport? Ask the children to make a list of appropriate verbs, such as 'fast', 'slow', 'hard', 'soft', etc.

Sentence construction and punctuation

1 Discuss how helpful the layout of the pages shown on the poster are for the reader. What features are used? *(Point out the use of bullet points, capital letters, dotted lines, etc.)* Can the children think of any other devices that might make it easier to use?

WORD Level
Spelling

1 Notice what changes, if any, happen to root words when the suffix '-ing' is added, e.g. 'jumping', 'canoeing' and 'wrestling'. The poster is good for stimulating work on syllabification, for example, 'bad/min/ton'. It is also good for looking for small words within longer words; for looking at compound words, e.g. 'football'; and for looking for common letter strings.

Vocabulary extension

1 Devise different ways to classify some of the sports, e.g. those played on your own, those with a team, those played in water, those played on a pitch of some sort, those played with one ball, or with more than one ball, etc. Do the children find some systems easier to use than others? Why? Can any of the systems be reviewed and refined?

Related texts:

'100 Greatest Sports Champions' by Donald Sommerville

'Sports and Games' by Neil Jameson

'True Sport Stories' by Tim Lardner

'I Wonder Why: Encyclopaedia' published by Kingfisher (excellent for young Key Stage 2 children)

Playing with Words

About the text

There are a variety of different examples of word play on this poster, from kennings (see point 3, Reading Comprehension), riddles and 'knock knock' jokes to puns.

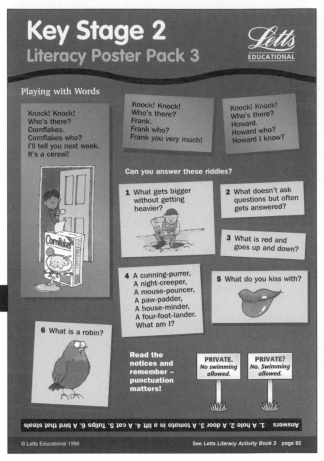

Teaching opportunities at:

TEXT Level
Reading comprehension

1 Read and enjoy the 'knock knock' jokes. Discuss why they are funny. What technique does the punch line use? *(Usually they are puns, i.e. a play on words, using words with similar sounds but different meanings for humorous effect.)* Ask the children for other 'knock knock' jokes they might know.

2 Look at riddles 1 and 2. These can be answered by the application of logic. Riddles 3, 5 and 6, however, are further examples of puns, or plays on words and require a more creative approach to answering them. Ask the children for further examples of both types of riddle.

3 Riddle number 4 is a different type. It is called a 'kenning'. Kennings originated in Old English and Norse. They are compound words which name something without using the actual name itself, so a 'death-bringer' is a sword.

4 The two signs are interesting uses of punctuation – and an apt reminder that punctuation can make a big difference to meaning!

Writing composition

1 Make a class collection of 'knock knock' jokes, perhaps keeping the answers in the back, or upside down. Can the children illustrate them without giving the game away?

2 Make a class collection of riddles.

3 Try making up some kennings on different subjects, perhaps animals or forms of transport. These can be tried out on family and friends – and then refined.

SENTENCE Level
Grammatical awareness

1 It is interesting to study each type of word play on the poster and analyse the use of pronouns. Notice which use the first-person, which the second-person and which the third-person. Notice with the punctuation boards that they are written as imperatives and the pronoun (you) is inferred rather than stated.

Sentence construction and punctuation

1 Punctuation is very important on the poster. Study how it is used and discuss why, especially with reference to the swimming pool joke. Ask the children to write their own warning signals, but to muddle punctuation to make it humorous.

WORD Level
Spelling

1 Look for the use of the apostrophe in contracted words on the poster. *('Who's', 'I'll' 'it's' and 'doesn't'.)* Discuss their extended forms and look in books for other examples. *('Who is', 'I will' 'it is' and 'does not'.)*

2 Find the word 'answer' in the poster and draw attention to the silent 'w' in it. Ask the children to suggest other words containing silent letters. *(There are many possible answers.)* Classify these according to silent letter.

Vocabulary extension

1 Use the word 'allowed' from the poster to discuss homonyms (words that sound the same but have different meanings). Discuss the difference between 'allowed' and 'aloud'. Allow this to lead into further work on homonyms, for instance, by asking the children to write sentences using the homonyms to indicate clearly the differences in meaning.

Related texts:

'Who's There?' illustrated by Tim Archbold (all the favourite 'knock, knock' jokes)

In the Library

About the text

This poster shows two children in a school library. It shows the arrangement of fiction books (alphabetically according to author) and includes a simple chart showing the Dewey classification of non-fiction books.

Teaching opportunities at:

TEXT Level
Reading comprehension

1 The contents of this poster are best discussed in the context of your own school library and its organisation and that of local libraries generally.

2 Ensure children understand the difference between fiction and non-fiction.

3 Why is it important to have some system of arranging books in libraries? Whose job is it to ensure books are correctly shelved and returned? *(It makes it easy to find the books. The librarian is in charge.)*

4 Discuss the way fiction books are usually arranged. Ask the children to identify where the two books the children are holding should go on the shelves. *('Alice in Wonderland' (Lewis Carroll) should go between 'On the Run' (Nina Bawden) and 'Birdspell' (Helen Cresswell) while 'Never Kiss Frogs' (Robert Leeson) should go between 'Stig of the Dump' (Clive King) and 'The Twig Thing' (Jan Mark).)*

5 Take a selection of fiction books and put them in a heap. Ask the children to arrange them in alphabetical order, according to author.

6 Discuss the Dewey classification system. Ask specific questions, such as where books on particular subjects would be found, etc. Compare this system with the system you have in your own school for organising non-fiction books.

Writing composition

1 Ask the children to write some simple rules of do's and don'ts for using your library. *(For example, putting books back, putting them in the right way round, keeping to alphabetical order, etc.)*

2 Ask the children to explain, in their own words, the system of organising both fiction and non-fiction books.

SENTENCE Level
Grammatical awareness

1 Take a selection of books from the school library shelf. Ask the children to note the use of powerful or persuasive words in the book blurbs and to classify these according to whether they are nouns, verbs or adjectives. Put the words into the relevant lists.

Sentence construction and punctuation

1 Analyse a selection of book titles. Note how and when capital letters are used. Give children a few book titles written without capitals and ask them to write them correctly (i.e. in both upper and lower case).

WORD Level
Spelling

1 Give children a range of common letter patterns and ask them to find words on the poster containing them, e.g. 'au', 'or', 'ur', 'al', 'ph', 'ion', 'ious', 'age', 'ogy'. *(For example, 'author', 'world', 'literature', 'hospitals', 'philosophy', 'religion', 'religious', 'language', 'technology'.)* Then ask them to suggest other words with the same letter patterns and check their spellings in a dictionary.

Vocabulary extension

1 Look up the names of some subjects listed in the Dewey classification list in a dictionary which provides information on word origins. This will provide a fascinating insight into how words have come about through history.

> ### Related texts:
>
> 'Once Inside the Library' by Barbara Huff (an excellent book explaining how a library works)
>
> NB Some libraries also have their own leaflets explaining what they offer, e.g. services, information packs, etc.

High frequency word lists

about
after
again
an
another
as

back
ball
be
because
bed
been
boy
brother
but
by

call(ed)
came
can't
could

did
dig
do
don't
door
down

first
from

girl
good
got

had
half
has
have
help

her
here
him
his
home
house
how

if

jump
just

last
laugh
little
live(d)
love

made
make
man
many
may
more
much
must

name
new
next
night
not
now

off
old
once
one
or
our
out

over

people
pull
push
put

ran

saw
school
seen
should
sister
so
some

take
than
that
their
them
then
there
these
three
time
too
took
tree
two

us

very

want
water
way
were
what
when

where
who
will
with
would

your

*Days of
the week*
Sunday
Monday
Tuesday
Wednesday
Thursday
Friday
Saturday

*Months of
the year*
January
February
March
April
May
June
July
August
September
October
November
December

*Common
colour
words*
black
white
blue
red

green
yellow
pink
purple
orange
brown

*Numbers
to 20*
one
two
three
four
five
six
seven
eight
nine
ten
eleven
twelve
thirteen
fourteen
fifteen
sixteen
seventeen
eighteen
nineteen
twenty

*Your name
and address*

*The name
and address
of your school*

Handy Hints for Learning to Spell New Words

LOOK
- Look carefully at the word.
- Does it contain any letter patterns you already know?
- Do you know any other words like it?
- Which is the most difficult part of the word?
- Do you know what the word means?

SAY
- Say the word to hear how it sounds.
- Is the word spelt as it sounds?
- Can you break the word into smaller parts?

COVER
- Cover the word and try to see it in your mind.

WRITE
- Write the word from memory.
- Try not to copy.

CHECK
- Check your spelling with the original.
- Compare them.
- If you got it wrong, try it again.

Handy Hints for Planning Stories

SETTING
● Where will your story take place?

– in a house?   – in a shop?   – in a wood?

– in a castle?   – in a hospital?   – in a cave?

– at the seaside?   – at school?   – at a fair?

               – somewhere else?

CHARACTERS
● Who will be in your story?

– Will they be humans?   – Will they be animals?

– Will they be monsters?   – Will they be something else?

● What will they look like?

● What sort of things will they do?

● What sort of things will they say?

STORYLINE
● What will your story be about ?

● How will it begin?

● What sort of things will happen in the middle?

● How will your story end?

– happily?   – sadly?   – amusingly?

– will you make it into a 'cliffhanger', leaving the reader wanting to know more?

Handy Hints for Handwriting

BEFORE YOU BEGIN

Are you sitting comfortably?

Are you sitting up straight?

● Have you got enough light?

Have you got a smooth surface to write on?

Have you sloped your paper slightly?

Have you got a suitable pen or pencil to write with?

Are you holding your pen or pencil in a comfortable way?

Can you see what you are writing?

WHEN YOU HAVE FINISHED

Is the writing neat?

Is it easy to read?

Does it 'sit' on the line?

Are all letters well-shaped?

Are the letters evenly sized?

Are any letters too tall or too small?

Are the descenders of any letters too long or curly?

Is there enough space between the words and letters?

Are all the joins well made?

Have you put capital letters in all the correct places?

Have you used punctuation marks correctly?

Handy Hints for Checking Your Writing

SENTENCES

Do your sentences make sense?

Is there anything you want to move or change?

Is there anything you can leave out to make it clearer?

PUNCTUATION

Have you punctuated it correctly with:

– capital letters, full stops, question marks, exclamation marks, speech marks and commas?

SPELLING

Have you checked for silly spelling mistakes?

Have you looked up any words you are not sure of?

HANDWRITING

Is your handwriting easy to read?

Or are you going to do your work on the computer?

PRESENTATION

Have you thought of a good title?

Are you going to illustrate your work?

– What sort of illustrations would be best? (pictures, diagrams etc)

– Where will you place the illustrations?

● In what form will you present your work?

– in an exercise book?

– on paper?

– as a zig-zag concertina book?

– in some other format?

Handy Hints for Using Punctuation Marks

Punctuation helps us make sense of what we read.
Punctuation marks make writing easier for us to understand.
They help us to read with expression.

full stop

A **full stop** tells you to stop. You have come to the end of a sentence.
Every sentence must begin with a capital letter.
The dog chased the postman.

question mark

A **question mark** tells you a question is being asked.
What is the time?

comma

A **comma** tells you to pause. It is also used to separate items in a list.
After eating his dinner, the old man had a sleep.
In her bag Mrs Jones had apples, pears, bananas and grapes.

exclamation mark

An exclamation mark is used when we feel strongly about something or are surprised.
Stop that thief!

speech marks

We use **speech marks** to show someone is speaking.
We write what the person says inside the speech marks.
Tom said, "I like to watch television in the evening."

Other Literacy Materials available from Letts Educational:

Reception *Poster Pack* and *Teacher's Book*
Year 1 *Poster Pack* and *Teacher's Book*

Year 2 Term 1 *Activity Book*
Year 2 Term 2 *Activity Book*
Year 2 Term 3 *Activity Book*

Year 2 *Poster Pack* and *Teacher's Book*

Year 3 *Activity Book*
Year 4 *Activity Book*
Year 5 *Activity Book*
Year 6 *Activity Book*

Year 3 *Poster Pack* and *Teacher's Book*
Year 4 *Poster Pack* and *Teacher's Book*
Year 5 *Poster Pack* and *Teacher's Book*
Year 6 *Poster Pack* and *Teacher's Book*

Coming soon:

Year 3 *Differentiated Activity Book – Sentence Level*
Year 3 *Differentiated Activity Book – Word Level*

Year 4 *Differentiated Activity Book – Sentence Level*
Year 4 *Differentiated Activity Book – Word Level*

Year 5 *Differentiated Activity Book – Sentence Level*
Year 5 *Differentiated Activity Book – Word Level*

Year 6 *Differentiated Activity Book – Sentence Level*
Year 6 *Differentiated Activity Book – Word Level*

For more information or a catalogue request call **Freephone 0800 216592**